199

D1223572

The
Most Wanted Man
in America

The
Most Wanted Man
in America

BY JOHN WILLIAM CLOUSER
also known as the Florida Fox

WITH DAVE FISHER

STEIN AND DAY/*Publishers*/New York

First published in 1975
Copyright © 1975 by John William Clouser and Dave Fisher
All rights reserved
Designed by David Miller
Printed in the United States of America
Stein and Day/*Publishers*/Scarborough House,
Briarcliff Manor, N.Y. 10510

Library of Congress Cataloging in Publication Data

Clouser, John William.
The most wanted man in America.

1.   Clouser, John William.   2.   Crime and criminals–
Correspondence, reminiscences, etc.   I.   Fisher, David,
1946-   II.   Title.
HV6248.C48A34   364.3[B]   74-26961
ISBN 0-8128-1771-0

To every father who has lost his sons, and to every lover who has lost his soul mate in the terror of the night, this book is dedicated.

J. W. C.

This book is based on fact, but some of the real names of persons and other personal details have been changed. If any pseudonyms resemble the names of any living persons, it is entirely a coincidence.

We gratefully acknowledge the assistance and support of Margy Simons Clouser, Ed Kirkland, Charles Cullom, James Siff, the Cornwalls—Astrid, Jim, and Bill—Cal Barber, David Whitlow, John Garcia, Jerry Gibbs, Sol Stein, Michaela Hamilton, Richard and Joanne Curtis, Joanne Blackwelder, Rita Elgar, the Fraternal Order of Eagles in Daly City, California, J. B. Godwin, Paul Cunningham, David Burnett, and Leonard and Connie Hirshfeld.

J. W. C.
D. F.

INTERSTATE STOLEN AUTOMOBILE
WANTED BY FBI
JOHN WILLIAM CLOUSER

FBI No. 229,125 C

25 L 1 R 000 8
L 1 U 000

ALIASES: Jack Clauser, John William Clauser, Jack W. Clouser, Chuck A. Williams

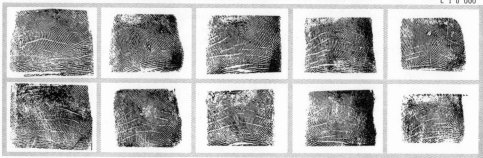

Photographs taken 1963

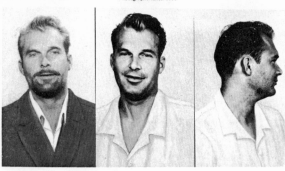

Jack William Clouser

DESCRIPTION

AGE: 32, born March 29, 1932, Chicago, Illinois
HEIGHT: 5'9"   EYES: blue
WEIGHT: 175 to 200 pounds   COMPLEXION: ruddy
BUILD: stocky   RACE: white
HAIR: blond (may be dyed black)   NATIONALITY: American
OCCUPATIONS: clerical worker, stock clerk
SCARS AND MARKS: tattoos, panther right shoulder, heart pierced by arrow left shoulder.
REMARKS: described as a weight lifter and has a knowledge of judo.

CAUTION

CLOUSER ESCAPED FROM A MENTAL INSTITUTION. HE ALLEGEDLY ASSAULTED ROBBERY VICTIMS AND CLAIMED HE WOULD NOT BE TAKEN ALIVE. REPORTEDLY IS AN EXCELLENT MARKSMAN AND IN POSSESSION OF A KNIFE. CONSIDER EXTREMELY DANGEROUS.

A Federal warrant was issued April 9, 1964, at Montgomery, Alabama, charging Clouser with interstate transportation of a stolen motor vehicle (Title 18, U. S. Code, Section 2312).

IF YOU HAVE INFORMATION CONCERNING THIS PERSON, PLEASE CONTACT YOUR LOCAL FBI OFFICE. PHONE NUMBER LISTED BELOW. OTHER OFFICES LISTED ON BACK.

Identification Order No. 3837
September 2, 1964

Director
Federal Bureau of Investigation
Washington, D. C.   20535

1 I turned the corner. My life as a fugitive would soon be over.

Right away one of the reporters in front of Tallahassee's Criminal Justice Building spotted me. He started running up the block, followed by at least two dozen other newspaper and television reporters and cameramen. The sky had turned almost black, getting ready to rain, and the cameramen turned their floodlights right in my face.

"Where you been, Jack?"

I smiled and kept walking.

"How you gonna plead?"

"Is it true you wrote insulting letters to J. Edgar Hoover?"

"What made you decide to give yourself up?"

The newsmen moved right along with me, shoving and shouting. At the advice of my attorney, who was walking alongside me step for step, I didn't answer any questions.

Two representatives of the Florida Criminal Justice Division were standing outside the building waiting for me. They were nice-looking young men, both a little nervous. The cameras, floodlights, and microphones were all aimed at them, and they carried out their duties like actors in a play.

"Mr. Clouser?" The first one had a soft southern accent.

"That's right," I said.

"I'm Special Agent Layman. This is Special Agent Harring. I have three writs for your arrest." He looked down and read from a handful of papers he was holding. "The first one is number nine-four-two-three-nine, dated third of April, 1964, charging you with conspiracy, bribery, kidnapping, aggravated assault."

That was the Cinema Theater.

"Second one is nine-six-four-o-two, charging you with breaking and entering with intent to commit a felony and grand larceny."

The gas station.

"The third one is nine-six-five-four-seven, dated third of April, 1964, charging you with conspiracy, robbery, assault to commit murder."

The liquor store.

"Not guilty to all charges," I said flatly.

"I am now placing you under arrest. You have the right to remain silent. You have the right to an attorney. . . ."

9

I raised my hands high in the air, as instructed. Special Agent Harring gave me a quick shakedown.

"If you will follow me, please," Agent Layman said.

I stepped in behind him. My attorney and Harring came next. As we walked the last few steps the reporters started shouting again.

We went into a sparkling clean men's room and I stripped for a complete search. Everything was done crisply, professionally, politely. These special agents were young and bright and almost friendly. Law enforcement in Florida had changed a lot since I wore a policeman's uniform.

After a short press conference, more pushing and shouting, one of the officers asked me to hold my arms out. With a split-second click-click, he snapped a pair of handcuffs on my wrists. I lifted my hands slightly and felt their weight.

"Let's go," he said, and we walked out into the rain.

The cameras were still spinning as we started the long drive to the Florida State Hospital at Chattahoochee, the mental hospital the whole thing started in. As we drove along I tried to look out and see how much things had changed physically. I already knew they hadn't changed too much politically. Northern Florida was still conservative country, and I was still a hated man.

On that August 21, 1974, Chattahoochee was as pretty as ever. Beautiful white buildings set on carefully grown plots of lush green grass and flowers. It could have passed as a resort, if you didn't know what went on behind the barred windows and locked doors.

At the hospital, nobody knew exactly what to do with me. With a local sheriff carrying all my belongings in a borrowed, broken, cardboard overnight bag, we went from building to building trying to find someone to take charge of me. I was as much a problem to the state of Florida in custody as I had been to the government of the United States while I was on the run.

As we left one reception building for what turned out to be our final destination, a nurse came running out after us. She was waving a folder and shouting, "A. W., A. W!"

The sheriff, A. W. himself, stopped and turned around. "What is it, Martha?"

"There's a note here attached to his records saying we should contact the FBI the minute we get him back." Then she paused and looked down at the folder she was holding. " 'Course," she continued, a little uneasily, "that note's been here for a long time."

That note had been there exactly ten years, four months, and nineteen days, ever since I took off into the Florida swamps to become America's most successful fugitive.

My name is John William Clouser. All my life I've been known as Jack, Jack Clouser, except to the federal government and the state of Florida, who knew me as the Florida Fox for the past ten and a half years. For most of that time I was on the FBI's top ten most wanted list. Since its inception in 1950, nobody has ever been on the most wanted list longer than me. For a long time I was the senior fugitive on the list. Number one, the most wanted man in America. And they never caught me.

The FBI brags that once placed on the top ten, a fugitive lasts an average of 147 days. I sure ruined their little average charts. They didn't capture me, and they didn't kill me. In 1973 I was taken off the list with no explanation or reason given. I have to assume it is because of the continuing embarrassment I caused to the bureau. I know for a fact that two agents were suspended because of me. And, as far as I've been able to find out, I'm the only person ever to be taken off the list alive and uncaptured.

Ten years. Almost four thousand days. Every single one of them spent being hunted by the finest, most modern law-enforcement agency in the world. Four thousand days living under assumed identities, constantly moving, always watching behind me, afraid even to tell the woman I married my real background.

My flight to stay free has taken me through forty-four states, all across Canada, up and down Mexico, and into twelve other foreign countries and territories. But in all that time, in all those places, I never robbed or stole a single thing since that first night I escaped, April 2, 1964.

The state of Florida said they wanted me for armed robbery. In fact, I was wanted as a showpiece, an ex-cop who got involved with the wrong people. I am not guilty of any of the crimes I was charged with. I swear to that. I *am* guilty of trying to set up a numbers operation, of numerous offenses while I was a cop, and of trying to beat the establishment. But most of all I was guilty of being a bigot, a man who used his muscles instead of his mind, and a man who believed that money could solve every problem.

My ten years on the run have changed me. I've learned about living with people, about people's feelings, about honesty, and about myself. My experiences have taught me how wonderful people can be, or how hateful, and that their skin color, their religion, or the amount of money in their pockets has nothing to do with it. I've learned the real importance of having a family, and how lonely it can be without one.

That was the hardest lesson of all.

Although I was born in Chicago, Illinois, in 1932, I was bred as a true son of the traditional South. For the first few years of my life we moved around, then we settled in Knoxville, Tennessee. My father was a civil sanitary hydraulic engineer, at first working for the Tennessee Valley Authority and later founding his own engineering firm. He was elected president of the Rotary Club of Knoxville. My mother was Lillian Lee Jackson, a descendant of Andrew Jackson. So the blood of a president of the United States runs in my veins.

My mother and father were good, bright, southern whites. And, as good southern parents are supposed to do, they raised me to be a racist. I was taught, like all my friends, that if you weren't a white Protestant, you were a second-class citizen. Being Catholic or Jewish was bad, but being black or brown was a whole lot worse. Colored people were inferior, even though they all had great rhythm and were good at manual labor.

I was always a gutsy kid and got into little jams now and then. One Halloween, for example, my little gang took our Boy Scout hatchets and knives and chopped this garden hose to pieces. We didn't know who lived there, but the next day on my way down to the bus stop I looked at the name on the mailbox: Lindsey Nelson. Lindsey Nelson is now one of the most famous sports announcers in the country, and at that point he was broadcasting the University of Tennessee football games. That didn't make him God, but it did make him a strong candidate for sainthood.

Because we lived right on a golf course I became a good golfer, but football was my real love. By the time I reached ninth grade I was the fastest runner on the squad, and I could dazzle them with legwork. My future was set as far as I was concerned—I'd star in high school, star at the university, marry a cheerleader, and play pro football. What else was there in life?

I made the varsity my sophomore year. One day in practice, when I replaced the first-string wingback to run plays, I got my leg crushed. The doctors wanted to operate but my father let me make my own

Upper left: Jack Clouser, at age nine, with pet bulldog Patty, at home in Knoxville, Tennessee. *Upper right:* Clouser on graduation from Central High School, Knoxville. *Below:* Clouser played in the 1959 Gator Bowl for the Orlando Jaycees.

decision. "I'll just see how it goes," I told the doctor. I was just too damn scared to have the operation. The leg healed and I did try to play football again, but I reinjured it almost immediately. In my junior year I had to give up football, the focus of my life, forever.

I took that bad, it changed me emotionally. Soon I picked up a reputation for being a bad kid. But I wasn't really bad, just a little wild. I got kicked out of school five times in one semester. For throwing books out the library window from the second floor. For trying to crash a social event with a counterfeit ticket (a teacher grabbed me and took me to the principal and I smashed him into a locker). For shooting dice in the toilet. For cutting school and hopping a freight train and going all over eastern Tennessee for four days. And I got kicked out for "immoral conduct" with the school floozy under the poinsettia bushes on the school grounds.

My first brush with the law happened right around this time. Myself and two friends decided to paint the monument in front of our rival high school with our own school colors, red and black. Unfortunately, the monument was actually a memorial to First World War soldiers. The Veterans' Administration started screaming that the monument had been defaced by Communist infiltrators. They offered a couple hundred dollars reward for the names of the people that had done this sneak attack. Eventually someone turned us in, and we ended up losing our drivers' licenses, being restricted to our homes for six months, and having a juvenile record. My relationship with my father was not too good to start with, he simply wasn't a very outwardly affectionate man, and this did nothing to help things.

Even with all my playing around, I managed to keep decent grades and entered the University of Tennessee. But I didn't last too long there, mainly because of a cute brunette named Judy Captain (a short version of a Greek name). Her father was a very popular guy who ran a Greek restaurant in Knoxville, and she was really a nice girl. She was excluded from sororities because of her background, and I was excluded from football because of my bad knee. We started going out together, two people looking for anything or anybody, and we eventually eloped.

There was really no way that marriage could have worked. We were just too young, too poor, and too immature. We tried. I got a job at a chain furniture store as an assistant office manager. But just as we were beginning to save some money we had a baby boy, Kurt Clouser. Things got very tough, and we didn't get along at all.

14

The furniture chain sent me to Orlando, Florida. I thought central Florida was as close to paradise as I would ever get—the lakes, the climate, the sun. But Judy missed her family and friends and wanted to leave. Finally, pregnant again, Judy just couldn't take it any more. She took our son and left. Eventually she informed me that she wanted a divorce.

I fought her and lost. She got everything we had—our house, our appliances, our furniture, and our two children. I never saw my son or my daughter again.

I was alone, my life was completely empty. I needed something to give it structure and meaning. After looking around for a short time, I decided to become either a policeman or a fireman. Both were good, steady jobs. Both provided adventure and excitement. Both meant a regular paycheck. And most important, they were jobs that provided both status and respect.

I don't really remember why I decided to become a cop, probably because I liked the uniform better. At that time I weighed about 158 pounds and my confidence was almost nonexistent. I figured being a cop would give me authority, power, and self-respect. So I joined the Orlando Police Department.

That turned out to be the worst mistake I ever made.

At first I was determined to be the best cop that ever walked a beat. I would be tough, but honest and friendly. Everyone on my beat would love me, and criminals would fear me. I would build a life for myself as a respected member of the community. It all seemed so easy.

I started out on the night shift, pounding a beat in the boondocks. I wasn't crazy about the hours or the area, but I felt pretty terrific about the way I looked in the uniform. I was also trying very hard to get in with the other policemen, to become one of the boys. That wasn't easy. The department was very tight, and any new man was looked at with great suspicion until he proved himself. It took me a few months until I got the right opportunity.

I was walking my new beat on the night shift, the downtown area, and I noticed some lights on in this garden furniture shop. I put my hand on my gun and carefully approached the building. I was following the procedure I had been taught, staying in the shadows, trying to get the drop on whoever was inside the shop. I did exactly that, until I saw who was robbing the place.

It was Mike Trestlee, a veteran officer, my superior in rank as well as years.

15

I walked up behind him and asked, as casually as I could, "Hey, Mike, how come you're stealing things off my beat?"

He jumped about seven feet straight into the air. But when he turned around and saw who had caught him, he made a nice soft landing.

"Oh, Jack," he said, really surprised to see me. "Don't worry about all this. Here, get in my car and take a ride with me."

And then he promptly drove me off my beat, clear across town to his home. There he unloaded everything, took me inside, woke his wife, introduced us, and had her fix us coffee.

The next day I didn't know what to do about Trestlee. Finally I decided to do the easiest thing, absolutely nothing. I knew I was wrong—but I also knew that I'd be an outcast, and risk my career, if I reported him. I just went back to my beat without a word to anyone.

Trestlee had a close friend on the force, a real he-man, Mr. Muscles type. A few days after the incident the guy came up to me and said, "Hey, Clouser, I got the word from Mike. He says you're all right. You didn't talk. You're a good guy."

I had proved myself.

Muscles took me under his wing and started teaching me the secrets of weight-lifting and body-building. In four months, with hard work and proper eating, I went from 158 pounds to 190. I was strong at 158, but at 190 I really thought I was something.

One night I was working the swing shift when a waitress came out of a bar and asked me to throw out some troublemaker. I figured that would be an easy job, until I walked into the place. Percy Jones, the toughest sonofabitch in Orlando, was laying across the bar.

I tried to do right by Percy. I walked up to him and said politely, "Excuse me, but there've been complaints about you. You mind stepping outside?"

Wham! He jumped up and hit me so hard I went flipping right over the counter to the floor. He came leaping over the counter right behind me and began stomping me and kicking me. I somehow got up and we fought up and down the whole place, even knocking some plaster right off the wall. He ripped my clothes off, my badge, my whistle, everything. But finally I got the advantage and I kicked his ass real bad. I ended up going to the tailor and he went to the hospital.

My reputation was made after that. Nobody hassled me any longer. In fact, the only problem I had on the force was with women.

They just wouldn't leave me alone. And that is meant as a complaint. Throughout my adult life my inability to stay away from women—and them from me—has been a major source of my problems.

While I was on the Orlando police force I used to stand on the corner of Central and Orange Avenues, just waiting. Often enough a woman would come along, touch my arms, feel my muscles, and actually shudder.

"Hi!" I'd say. "How you doing? I'm Jack Clouser. I get off at eleven P.M. Could I pick you up and take you somewhere?"

They usually said yes. Soon as I was off from work, I'd pick them up in the car, stop at the package store and get a six-pack, drive out to the orange groves, take the blanket out, and do whatever came naturally.

Over and over and over this happened. It makes me sound like a braggart, but it's true. I've always had more women than was good for me.

I got married for the second time about a year after Judy left me. My wife's name was Shirley and she was a beautiful local girl. I really never gave her a chance. All I wanted from her was children to replace the son and daughter I had lost. But she couldn't give me any, something was wrong with her and she couldn't get pregnant. We lived together six months, got married, stayed together four more months, and then divorced. She later told me she was going to marry an airman from Pinecastle Air Force Base.

"Go ahead," I told her. "I don't care."

And I didn't. I had so many women that losing a wife meant nothing to me.

My life in Orlando at this time was terrific. Being a policeman was every bit as great as I'd hoped it would be. I was really respected, I liked the feeling of authority I had, and it seemed like more of an adventure than a real job. When I wasn't on duty there seemed to be an endless supply of women, booze, and parties. Everything was wonderful.

Before I found out how hard it is to resist temptations when you're a cop.

2

For almost two years I worked at being an honest policeman. It wasn't easy. So many temptations were constantly being thrown at me, it was tough to continue resisting. And, just like on so many other police forces in the country, not all my fellow officers did resist. There was no general organization like there is in some big cities, where lots of people share in the take. Instead, those cops who wanted to make a little extra money did so quietly and on their own. It was all small-time stuff—a two-dollar shakedown, disappearing garden furniture, a few bottles of liquor, a bribe for a bad memory—whatever the individual cop could put together for himself.

I had a small group of friends on the force and I stuck pretty close to them. I didn't blame anyone for taking all he could get—at that time my pay for working six days a week was $275 *a month*—but I decided to keep my own nose clean. I didn't care what anybody else did, but I was fanatical about staying honest. I liked my reputation as the toughest, maybe even the meanest cop on the force, and I wouldn't do anything to jeopardize it.

Though I prided myself on being tough, I also tried to be fair. I never, ever hurt anybody more than absolutely necessary. Once I caught a black burglar inside a store and took him in. Other men on the force gave me a lot of heat. "What'd you bring him in for?" they asked me. "Why didn't you shoot him up first?" Maybe I didn't like blacks in those days, but I didn't go around killing them.

I was still determined to have a successful career as an honest police officer. I even went to most of the extra classes the department offered. I studied judo, and because it made me tougher I loved it. Going to judo class reminded me of going to football practice so long ago. I also became a drunkometer expert, qualified to administer the alcohol-content test to people suspected of driving while intoxicated.

One night I investigated an accident and ended up arresting the man who caused it. He had been drinking, but I didn't believe he was drunk. I decided to give him the test. This guy was so scared of losing his license he pulled a $20 bill from his wallet and offered it to me.

That did it! Now I had to convict him. If I didn't, I was afraid I'd be accused of taking a bribe, even though I never touched his money. I tested him three different times, fiddled with the machine the third time, and finally failed him. Then I arrested him for drunken driving and attempted bribery. That's how strict I was in those days.

But slowly I changed. No matter how I tried to stretch it, that $275 monthly just didn't last. Particularly after I got married for the third time.

I just couldn't seem to stay single. No sooner was Shirley out of my life than June Moore Datilio entered it. She was a stunning redhead with a fantastic body that everybody in the department was desperate to get their hands on, but nobody could get anywhere with her. It became an ego thing with me and I went after her. She was working as a meter maid and one night we went up to the police camp at a nearby lake. Wow! What a time we had! Not too long afterward, we got married.

At first things were fine. We were happy together awhile and when she told me, "We're pregnant," I was overjoyed. All I wanted in life was another son. She gave him to me. Charlton Anthony Clouser.

After Tony was born, things got very bad. June spent every penny I could make, at first all the legal money, later everything I could steal. She was also insanely jealous of me. If I came home fifteen minutes late from work she'd accuse me of getting a quickie. Once I came home two hours late; the police department softball team won the championship and we were out celebrating. When I walked in the door she was standing there pointing my own service revolver in my face. I thought sure she was going to kill me, but she ended up just smashing me across the head and leaving a lump as big as a fist.

I was afraid of her and I loved her and I hated her. This was not the best relationship a man and a woman have ever had. And it was at least partially because of my need to "prove" myself to her that I became a crooked cop.

It started innocently enough. One night I stopped a car going the wrong way on a one-way street and discovered the driver was smashed-out-of-his-mind drunk. I took him to the station and charged him.

Within an hour a prominent Orlando attorney showed up and said, "Do you know who you arrested? This is Mr. ———." He named a rich local landowner. "Can you make an exception?"

"No," I said, "the law is for everyone." At the time I really believed that.

Mr. Fixit, his attorney, took me aside. "Don't be so bullheaded, young man," he said. "Instead of getting up there in court and saying, 'This man was definitely drunk and driving the wrong way down a one-way street,' just get up and say, 'I stopped him for driving the wrong way on a one-way street and he appeared to have been drinking. I offered him a drunkometer test; he refused it, so I charged him.' If you do this I promise you that you will not be sorry."

I testified exactly as Mr. Fixit asked. The judge found his client guilty of driving the wrong way on a one-way street and innocent of drunk driving. Within forty-eight hours I received an envelope in the mail. Wrapped inside a piece of paper was a $50 bill. Fifty bucks! That was the easiest money I ever made, and with June's spending I needed it more than ever. Right then I gave up all my pretensions about being an honest cop. I started doing my thing.

My thing was shaking down every black in my district that I could find. I knew there was no way I could get in trouble. I was only robbing blacks, and that was almost legal in the South. It wasn't like stealing from a white person at all. I began by rolling drunks. I even had a regular, a man named Joe Robinson. Every Friday he got paid and every Friday night at midnight I'd find him on the same corner, stone drunk, talking to the trees. "Joe," I would tell him, "you're under arrest, get in the car." I'd stick my hand in his pocket and take what was left of his paycheck and then become a nice guy and let him go. I must have rolled him two dozen times.

Besides my shakedowns, I got close to the local bootleggers. Any time I was short of money I'd just head right down to their hangout. "Edward," I'd explain to the leader, "I guess we'll have to arrest you for having all this illegal booze here." I'd go right to the hole in the wall behind the tapestry and start confiscating the evidence.

"Go right ahead, Mr. Jack," he'd answer me, "you go ahead and take that."

Then I would pause and play my role perfectly. "Edward, am I going to have to take you in, or will you be satisfied for me just to take the booze?"

"Just take it, Mr. Jack, and forget all about me."

We forgot about each other. I took the booze and sold it to friends, neighbors, anyone willing to pay a fair price for it.

And finally there was guns. This was in 1958 and 1959 and the Cuban Revolution was in full swing. I knew somebody who was willing to buy every weapon he could find and then shipped them to Cuba. I became a steady supplier. I confiscated every piece I could find—handguns, rifles, shotguns—and I even went so far as to take weapons from armories.

20

And all the money I ever made, June found a way to spend and still come up a little short. Fidel Castro doesn't know it, but he has June Clouser to thank for at least a little of the success of his revolution.

June and I continued to get along about as well as Castro and Batista. We would fight all the time, and with us it was just as often physical as verbal. Finally neither of us could take it any more. She took our son and all our furniture and appliances and split. I couldn't believe it when I walked into my house and saw I was wiped out for the second time. This was getting silly. I was tired of buying new toasters.

Eventually June and I reconciled. We couldn't get along together, but we just kept coming back for more. Soon after we started living together again she told me she was pregnant. This time I didn't believe it was my child, but boy, was I wrong! When that baby was born he looked more like me than any of my other three children. We named him Timothy Makum and he was adorable. No matter what bad times June and I had, she gave me two sons, and I never forgot that.

We were managing to survive with my paycheck and what I could steal, and we got a real boost when I was promoted to sergeant. Most men don't make sergeant in fifteen years, some of them never make it. I made it in four years and ten months! As a sergeant there were four possible assignments: motorcycles, regular patrol, desk work in the station, and the detective bureau. I wanted to be a detective, for one very simple reason.

That's where the most money was to be made.

One of the biggest underworld activities going on in Orlando then was bolita, the numbers. The numbers works simply. You bet any money on any number, 1 to 100. If that number wins for the week the payoff is usually about sixty times what you bet. There is an incredible amount of money to be made running a numbers operation. But since people usually don't bet too much, in order to run a profitable game you have to have a big organization of people picking up bets for you. These people quickly get known to the police, and the police have to be taken care of financially.

I wanted to be taken care of. And from the way the force was set up, I figured the easiest way for me to get in on the action would be as a member of the detective squad.

Unfortunately, the department chief decided to put me on the motorcycle squad. I had never even ridden a motorcycle, the last thing in God's world I wanted to do was be a motorcycle sergeant, and I didn't hesitate to tell other men in the department.

That was a mistake. There was another sergeant who did not like me very much named Ronnie Redmon. Ole Sergeant Redmon wrote a report to the chief saying that I was badmouthing the motorcycle squad. The chief decided I wasn't fit to be any type of sergeant and tried to bust me.

I never backed away from a fight with another man. I took the chief to the Civil Service Board and we had a big hearing. The result was that I was reprimanded for "talking loosely," but kept my job. The chief had no choice but to send me to the Detective Bureau. I was on my way to fortune!

It was a very short trip, and there was no pot of gold at the end. I lasted about five months as a detective, then my career as a defender of the law came to an abrupt end. The cause of it all was a friend of mine named George Fogel.

George Fogel was probably the most successful hustler in Orlando. He seemed to know just about everybody of importance on both sides of the law. He had promised me that, at the right time, he would introduce me to the head of the organized crime family in that area. That sounded good to me. But besides his contacts, I didn't know very much about George Fogel. I didn't know, for example, that he was running one of the biggest abortion rings in the country.

It turns out the police had been trying to nail Georgie for years. They were watching him carefully, and among other evidence they piled up were pictures of me parking the police car, while I was in uniform, in front of his office. They naturally figured I was involved in his abortion ring.

One night they trapped him good and busted him. If I had known the bust was coming I probably would have warned him, he was a personal friend, but it came as a total surprise to me. The only thing I did for him was make an anonymous phone call to his lawyer explaining what happened. Georgie eventually got seven years in the state penitentiary.

After he was busted I was called into the district attorney's office. They wanted me to admit I'd been part of this abortion ring, that I knew all about it and was protecting it. None of this was true. The only hard evidence they had were their photographs, and those pictures proved absolutely nothing.

But they had gotten to some of Georgie's women and got statements from them admitting they had sexual relations with me. Normally those would just be embarrassing, but in my case they were dangerous.

"We're going to bring your wife in here," one of the assistant D.A.s told me, "and show her all these statements about all your affairs."

Now, that shook me. I was really afraid of what June might do if she got angry enough.

Finally the D.A.'s office offered me a deal. They would do nothing about the statements if I quietly resigned from the police force. I jumped at the opportunity.

I know it's difficult to believe that a man could be so afraid of his wife that he'd quit his job rather than have her find out about his playing around. But in my case it was true. I was just terrified of June.

She wasn't thrilled when I came home and told her I was no longer a detective sergeant. She was very upset that I lost the power and the potential money. Besides, we were just barely scraping by as it was. Without my pay there was no way we could survive. I had to find some way to make a living, and I really didn't care what it was. I tried to figure out who I knew that might be able to help me. Georgie was going to jail, he wouldn't be any help. The people on the force certainly couldn't do too much for me. That left one person, my old buddy Mike Trestlee.

Mike had resigned from the police force about a year earlier and gone into business for himself. The same day I handed in my resignation I stopped in to see him.

"You all through down there, right?" he said.

"Right."

"Ain't nobody after your ass, right?"

"Right."

"O.K. I'm going to send you to some people that's going to take care of you. They gonna show you a new way. Don't worry about nuthin', you gonna be in good shape."

"Whatever you can do I'd sure appreciate," I told him. "And I'm not going to forget you helped me out."

I felt much better after seeing him. At least his promise would keep June happy for a few days. We had been getting along very well for awhile. She was still spending up a storm, but our fights were fewer and less ferocious.

The following Saturday morning, while June and I were eating breakfast, Mike Trestlee showed up. A few minutes later a big Cadillac pulled up in front and two guys got out of the car and came into the house. That was the first time I ever met Donald Marshall and Allie Brown. Then another car came up and Tim Peterman came in.

Trestlee introduced me to everyone, then Marshall took over. He explained that he was interested in starting a bolita operation, and he suggested that he might have a job for me. All he wanted to see was a copy of my resignation from the department.

After awhile they all left except Trestlee. We were sitting at the kitchen table and he said matter-of-factly, "Well, you know, those guys are real big in the underworld."

"Really?" I asked. This was better than I hoped.

"Haven't you seen the morning paper yet?" he said.

I hadn't even opened it up.

He took it and pointed out a story about the robbery of a local movie theater. The manager and a ticket clerk had been held up by two men with stockings over their heads, and all the receipts were stolen. "Well, those are the guys that knocked this place over last night," said Trestlee.

It was hard to believe anyone could sit at my table and tell me calmly that my new friends were armed robbers. "Is that right?" I asked.

"Yeah. You're dealing with big company."

I really was impressed. Good, bad, legal, illegal, none of that made any difference to me any more. These people were going to help me get some money and that's all I wanted to know.

We started working on the bolita ring. Besides me, Marshall, Brown, and Peterman, there was Toby Thomas, Peterman's working partner, and another man by the name of Kenny Diamond. We went around to the colored parts of Orange County, the ghetto and the country, and contacted various people that he knew and some people that I knew, and attempted to get this thing working. Technically this is known as conspiracy to commit illegal gambling and is very illegal. It is the only crime I was guilty of the entire time I was involved with these people. And we didn't even get the operation going! We had a real hard time finding anybody to work with us, because nobody believed Marshall had permission from the organization. It turned out that he didn't. Had I known that then, I would have dropped him like a hot potato.

We were all spending a lot of time together. One of the guys had rented a big house in a secluded area, and we did a lot of partying there. These people accepted me warmly, and it really meant something to me to be liked.

All the time we were working on the bolita operation, Peterman and Thomas were burglarizing homes and stores and bringing their stolen goods to the house for safekeeping. I saw the loot, I heard them talking about armed robberies they had committed.

At one point I asked Marshall if it wasn't dangerous being involved with Peterman and Thomas.

"Well," he answered, "we have to have operating money. We got to pay our runners and get everything set."

I accepted that as a worthwhile risk.

But then we got into some problems. Peterman and Thomas got a load of guns, rifles, shotguns, and pistols, from a gun shop. With the counterrevolution in full swing in Cuba, these guns were very valuable. Marshall, Trestlee, and Kenny Diamond decided to double-cross the burglars and cut them out of the deal completely.

Allie Brown and I were very upset. We knew this could blow anything else we had planned. It was obvious the whole thing was falling through. Our little outlaw group broke up, and that was the end of the bolita operation.

It wasn't the end of my association with these people, though. The police had learned I was hanging around with known criminals, and they probably really believed I was involved in all their illegal activities. They still felt cheated because they hadn't been able to connect me with the abortion ring. Plus an ex-cop involved with underworld characters made them all look bad.

They wanted my ass.

They got their first break when Toby Thomas was captured in the middle of a burglary, and for some reason I don't know he implicated his friend Tim Peterman. The police started following Peterman and discovered he was having an affair with the wife of a former football player who lived in the area. This gave the police something to work with.

"We understand your association with professional criminals," they told Peterman, "and we also know that Jack Clouser is involved.

We want him bad, and you're going to help us or we're going to tell You-Know-Who that you're screwing his wife. He'll probably kill you."

They gave Peterman some time to think about that. Originally he gave a statement saying that Marshall, Diamond, and Trestlee had robbed the Cinema Theater the day before I ever met them. The cops wouldn't accept that. They wanted me, and they wanted Allie Brown because of his reputation as a muscleman and troublemaker. They persuaded Peterman to change his testimony from Marshall, Diamond, and Trestlee to Marshall, Clouser, and Brown. Then they offered Trestlee a deal—he'd go free if he corroborated Peterman's testimony. Trestlee had the choice of going to jail or staying a free man. It couldn't have been a difficult decision to make.

My explanation of the way the case shaped up might sound like paranoia. But I swear, where the Cinema Theater was concerned, I was an innocent man. Not necessarily a good man, or an honest man, or even an intelligent man. But in this case, innocent.

Of course, the testimony changes were going on in the back of the police station, and I didn't know anything about it then. I learned all that later, from a friend on the force.

Meanwhile, my family would get telephone calls all night long. At daybreak we'd hear a car pull up in front of the house and then hear guns being fired into our front yard. June was terrified.

I figured it had to be Trestlee and Marshall doing this, that they were mad at me for siding with Peterman and Thomas after the gun job. But I never did find out for sure.

Things got worse and worse. Gunshots, garbage thrown in our yard, firecrackers, constant harassment. June finally couldn't take it any more.

"The hell with this," she screamed at me. "You're going to get me out of here right now, today, or I'm taking the boys and leaving!"

She was right, there was nothing to stick around for. So I hired a trailer and we packed up all the small things that we could save and took off for Tampa.

I was on the run for the first time in my life. It was a very, very small beginning.

3 We didn't make a very good fugitive family. I hand-painted my white convertible black and started using the name C. A. (for Charlton Anthony) Williams, my very first alias. We didn't even bother changing the license plate number because it wasn't the cops I was worried about, it was Trestlee and Marshall.

I went into an employment agency in Tampa, made up a story about just getting out of the service, and they sent me out to a shopping center for a job as an assistant clerk. Nobody at the shopping center asked any questions or bothered to check my phony references. That was what the agency was supposed to do. The agency wanted the fee so bad, they just sent me out without checking. Later, when I was on the run, it turned out to be an important discovery.

While I was hiding in Tampa the big roundup came in Orlando. Everybody was arrested except me, and when they couldn't find me they put a warrant out for my arrest. I was picked up in Tampa, while I was on my way home from Clearwater Beach. Some sharp police officer spotted my unchanged license plate number.

I was charged with armed robbery, but no one told me exactly what robbery. I wasn't too worried because I knew it had to be a mistake. They put me in the Clearwater jail and about six hours later Harvey Doan of the Orlando Police Department showed up with a big smile on his face.

"You want to confess here or back in Orlando?" he asked.

"I got no idea what you're talking about," I told him, and I didn't. "What are the charges?"

"You don't know? Shit."

"I don't know nothing. They didn't tell me nothing here."

"Jack, we got you for the Cinema Theater armed robbery."

The Cinema Theater job! I couldn't believe it. I didn't even meet the people who did it until the day after it happened! I told Doan he was crazy, I didn't have the slightest connection with that robbery.

"You're a goddamned liar, Jack," he said. "We got you good this time." Then he laughed. Right there I realized I was in for some deep trouble. I just kept my mouth shut, and didn't give him a speck of trouble on the way home.

Overnight I became a celebrity. The robbery was one of the biggest crimes in Orlando in awhile, and when an ex-cop was indicted

27

the story became front-page news. I was in the headlines almost every day, and those local papers tried me and convicted me and did everything except pull the lever on the electric chair.

The week before the trial started somebody from the district attorney's office offered me a deal. If I would plead guilty to the armed robbery charge and testify against Brown and Marshall, they would only give me five years in the state penitentiary. Big deal! Five years for something I didn't do. It was silly. I refused.

My trial was a complete farce. The only testimony against me came from Peterman and Marshall, who were out to save their own skins. The people who were "kidnapped" and robbed looked me right in the eye and said, "He doesn't look anything like the man who robbed me."

I knew my only chance was to testify for myself. I begged my attorney to let me on the stand, but he refused. "If you're going to say you hadn't met those people yet, what's the sense? Nobody's gonna believe you anyway."

I was convicted and sentenced on a Sunday morning. It was a heavy dose: thirty years for armed robbery, ten years for kidnapping without ransom, five years for aggravated assault, five years for conspiracy. A total of fifty years, to run concurrently with the thirty-year sentence.

As I walked out of that courtroom, in shock, I muttered, "You play a man's game, you gotta take a man's punishment."

The reporters quoted me and made it sound like I was confessing to the crime. I wasn't, I was thinking that what I got was my own fault for hanging around people I knew to be bad. I did associate with these people; I did try to get into organized bolita. But I never robbed anybody—after I left the police department, of course.

Allie Brown was sent down to the farm, the chain gang, and Donald Marshall and I went to the Raiford State Penitentiary. Raiford was never too bad. I worked as a clerk-typist in the chaplain's office. We had our own television set in our four-man cell. The food was edible. And the fact that I was still one tough-looking sonofabitch, and a convicted armed robber, guaranteed that no one would try to push me around.

The most difficult part of prison was the mental anguish. I never went through such hell in my life, to see my sons on the visitors' days and hear them ask, "When are you coming home, Daddy? Why are you up here?"

Then I would get the usual prison grapevine stories. "Your wife's screwing this guy, your wife's shacking up with So-and-So, your wife left here and went to a motel with the guy who drove her up." Everyone tells you different stories about who's doing what to your woman. Whether it's true or not, it drives you crazy.

About the only relief I had came from a local do-gooder who would visit my cell at Raiford. We'd sit and talk about my family, the boys in particular. A friend of his ran a summer camp in another small Florida town, and he asked if I'd permit them to spend some time there. Permit them! I was really grateful. As long as I was inside there was absolutely nothing I could do to help my sons. This guy was offering me the opportunity to make sure they had some fun. I sent him to see them, feeling happy to do something nice for them. Knowing they were able to have fun helped me live through the long, lonely days behind bars.

The main topics of conversation inside a prison are women, getting out, gambling, dope and liquor, and women. The men in Raiford used to make a mess of what they called "prison buck," a semi-alcoholic drink that they fermented. They always cut me in for a few cups. I also could have all the pills and dope I wanted, but I was really against any sort of drugs. I'd always been an athlete and I thought too much of my body to risk ruining it with dope. My only real vice inside was gambling, and there was never a problem finding some action. There was always a game of something going on, and the legal tender, the payoffs, were cigarettes. I didn't smoke, and I played a mean hand of poker, the result being a locker filled with cigarettes. This is how I paid for my legal help.

No one in jail believes he is there permanently. Everybody is constantly looking for the way out, everybody always has a plan. I started looking to get out the first day I was in. I didn't feel I had a fair trial and I wanted to appeal. I just didn't know how to go about it. I turned to another inmate for help.

Christopher S. Kelly was an incredibly brilliant man. He had been the driver of the car in a robbery-murder and was in for a long stretch. We played a lot of poker and I beat him pretty good. I let him work off his debt by helping me with my legal work; the time I didn't beat him for I paid off in cigarettes. We had illegal copies of law books hidden all over the prison—one in the school, another in the church, and another behind the pipes in one of the cells. We would just write and write, trying everything.

I wasn't the only inmate Kelly was helping. Clarence Gideon was a little old gray-haired man, a shoemaker from Miami who had been convicted of robbing a rinky-dink pool hall. He had appealed his conviction on the grounds that he had not been represented by an attorney because he couldn't afford to hire one, and his appeal went all the way to the United States Supreme Court.

One afternoon Old Man Gideon and me and a few other inmates, the ones who had kept out of trouble and could be trusted to leave the cell block, were sitting around on the curb, across from the canteen. A guard came out and told Gideon the captain wanted to see him. He walked inside.

Fifteen minutes later he came out and he was literally jumping into the air in happiness. In a landmark decision, *Gideon* v. *Wainwright* (Wainwright was the Florida prison system director), the Supreme Court overturned his conviction. I was watching history being made. After that I felt pretty damn good about my young legal helper.

Marshall and I took a pauper's oath and obtained a thick transcript of our trial. We studied and studied, with Kelly's help, and finally found an error. At one point in our trial the district attorney had asked the jury, "Why didn't So-and-So's wife testify that he had done such-and-such a thing?" You simply cannot tell a jury how a particular defendant should have testified. It's illegal. The Court of Appeals agreed with us, and finally set a date for our release pending a new trial. After more than two years in prison, I was going to be a free man again.

My release didn't come through right away, and during my waiting period I received one of the most incredible offers of my life. It came from the first true revolutionary I ever met, a little guy we called the Sheik because he was in prison for bigamy. Prison wasn't easy for him. Because of his far-out political and religious beliefs he was really hated, and there was always somebody trying to pick a fight with him. I liked this little dude and I gave him my protection, so nobody would mess with him. At times that made both of us outcasts, and I spent dozens of interesting hours talking to this guy.

One day we were sitting in my cell and he asked, "When you get out on bond, can you wait five or six months? Then I'll be out and I'm going to take you with me to Cuba. We'll go to the guerrilla school that Castro runs down there."

"Man, are you kidding?" I asked him. "Can you really get us into a thing like that?"

"Absolutely," he answered, "no question about it. We'll go down there and be trained and come back to Florida and cause some real problems."

The Sheik had some intelligent ideas, but this plot sounded like something from junior G-men to me. Jesus, I'm thinking to myself, I'm sure disgusted with the state of Florida, thirty years for a crime I didn't commit. But go to Cuba and come back and be a traitor to my country? No, I can't, there's no way I can do that. I got the blood of a president in my veins.

But I'm still thinking, and I come up with another idea: Do I have the balls to go down there and *pretend* to be a traitor? Then come back and tell Uncle Sam what I find out? I could tell Castro's men that I got thirty years unjustly from Florida. And I was responsible for guns getting to Fidel. I could make it work. And afterward, the U.S. government would be so grateful they'd make sure all charges against me were thrown out.

I decided it was worth a try. I would go to the government when I was let loose and offer them my services. It really did seem like a romantic adventure. And finally I saw it as a chance to do some good for my country and maybe try to make up for all the rotten shit I did as a policeman.

My mother put up my bail money, $2,500, and the bond itself was written by an old friend, then working as a bondsman for a new company. At last, I was out.

I took a deep breath of free air and headed right for the trailer camp to see my family. The first person I saw was my son Timmy. He came up to me and said, "Are you my daddy?"

I told him I was.

He hauled off and punched me right in the stomach. "Don't you leave me any more," he said.

"Son, I'll try not to," I told him.

I went inside to see June. She seemed really glad to see me, and we talked for a long time. Then I opened the drawer to put my meager little amount of clothes away. That's when I noticed everything gone. My rifle, my golf clubs, my tennis racket, all my clothes, all my furniture and appliances, either sold or given away. I was completely wiped out for the third time.

That wasn't the only shock. I opened a closet and the first thing I saw was a man's jacket with the name "Paul" sewed on it. I held it up. "Who the fuck is this?"

June was really embarrassed. She admitted Paul was some hardware dealer she had been going out with. I didn't know what to say.

"I'm glad you're out," she said, breaking the heavy silence. "You're my husband I love you. From now on, I'll really try to be a good wife."

That was all I wanted to hear. I agreed to at least try to forget it. Besides, I had other things on my mind. I wanted to go to Cuba!

My problem was how to arrange it. After really thinking about it I contacted an old college acquaintance who had become an FBI agent in Tennessee, and I gave him the whole story.

"All I ask," I said, "is that you get to Mr. Hoover, tell him the story, and then cut me loose. If I survive I'll have the whole story when I get back. If I die in Cuba, then I die. I'm not afraid to try it."

The agent was skeptical. "I've heard dozens of plans just like this one, and none of them has ever worked out," he said. Finally I persuaded him to at least give me a chance. "O.K.," he agreed, "we'll report this to Mr. Hoover. You'll get an answer."

I went back to our house in Orlando to wait. It wasn't an easy time. Somehow, my past record was always being discovered when I went for a job. After I was fired from two different places I gave up the thought of earning a living. We weren't too hard up for money because we were staying with the widow of a very close friend of mine from the department. For the entire summer, I played father to my two sons and my dead friend's three sons. It was one of the most wonderful summers of my life. By September I began to get really nervous. I hadn't heard from the FBI, and the D.A., Jim Russ, was getting ready to put me back on trial. I decided to go and see him, to talk man to man.

"Now, look, Mr. Russ," I started, "I know I'm a very controversial issue. But, I swear to this, I didn't commit that crime. I didn't even know those other people when that theater was robbed."

I told the D.A. the story, and as much as he hated me and as much as he knew I hated him, he was genuinely surprised. "Why didn't you testify you didn't meet them until the day after?" he asked, or something to that effect.

"My attorney wouldn't let me get on the stand. I wanted to, I really wanted to."

He looked me right in the eye. "Who really committed the robbery?"

I couldn't answer that. "I could tell you this guy or that guy, but it's only hearsay."

32

District Attorney Russ really didn't know exactly what to do. "Did you commit any crime when you were with that group?"

"Yeah," I said, "just like I told you. Conspiracy for bolita. That's all."

"What about the gas station job?"

"What gas station job?"

"The Hurricane Gas Station was robbed. You know anything about it?"

"All I know is that I didn't have anything to do with it."

He nodded. "O.K., we'll try to investigate this and then we'll check back with you."

I left, but I didn't trust him at all. He'd been trying to convict me for too long. I couldn't believe all of a sudden he was going to help me beat my problem.

I was right. A few days later another assistant called and offered me a deal. "We're willing to drop the armed robbery charges," he explained, "but you're going to have to come down here and plead guilty to breaking and entering the Hurricane Service Station."

I blew my top. "You're full of shit!" I screamed at him. "Take your goddamn service station and stick it!"

That night two carloads of Orange County deputies showed up at the house armed with shotguns, took me downtown, and charged me with the burglary of the Hurricane Gas Station. I was so incredibly mad, I could have eaten the bars out of the maximum security cell. I'd sat in prison two years. If they wanted to charge me with a burglary, they should have laid it on me then. But not now, when I had my freedom.

Back in jail, I couldn't even get bail. My old buddy had stolen all the money from his bonding company and took off. It took me three weeks to find someone to put up the money.

I'm really upset now. I have no money. I can't earn a living. The police are hounding me. The newspapers are writing about me like I was a dangerous murderer. All my life I had been able to control my emotions and get through one difficult period after another. Now I was on the verge of blowing completely. All I needed was one little push.

I got more than a push, I got a whole shove, when I asked my five-year-old son Tony how he liked the summer camp I arranged for him to go to.

"Daddy," he said, "Mr. Bobby tried to play with my pee-pee."

"What?" Bobby was the guy who ran the camp.

"Yeah," Tony said very seriously. "Timmy's too. We ran away from him."

That pushed me over the line. I started throwing chairs against the walls, smashing lamps, turning over tables. I started calling people I knew, pleading with them. "I need a gun, I need a gun, I need a gun."

June saved me that time. She called her brothers and some friends and they came over and kept me right there. "Jack, you can't go up there and kill a man. All the trouble you're in now, you think you're going to go up there with a gun? Wait, man, wait until this is all behind you, then you can settle everything."

Finally some semblance of reason returned to me. They were right, I was in too much trouble to do the slightest wrong thing. Still, I felt terrible. At that point in my life I thought every homosexual was a deviate nut and should be killed. I don't believe that any more. Consenting adults should have the right to do whatever they want. But to try to abuse two kids, that's just too much.

I stayed as calm as I could for the next few days, but inside I was like a smoldering volcano, just ready to erupt. It was June who finally set me off. She kept harping and nagging, "Goddamn it, we're living in this attic. We're starving. Go out and get some money!"

"How? You tell me, how? I've tried to get a job. I've tried to borrow. How can I get some money?"

"You sonofabitch. You fucking weakling. I'm going to show you how to get money." She stomped out of the house.

She was back in less than two hours. "Here," she screamed, throwing two ten-dollar bills at my feet. "Feed your family."

I didn't know who the money came from, but it didn't make any difference. It was just the last straw. I was beaten. I couldn't even feed my family. I couldn't take any more.

I needed to escape from my problems. If I could have found liquor I would have started drinking. Instead I found marijuana and pills and I got into them. It was the first time in my life I had ever smoked; and I smoked two joints by myself. Then I hit the pills: uppers, downers, red, yellow jackets, one after another I swallowed them down. I had to shut my mind. My kids, my wife, the harassment of the police department, being charged with a crime two years after it was committed because I wouldn't plead guilty to something I hadn't done, it was all too much.

I managed to drive to Pine Hills to see a man I knew from prison.

He was the drug connection at Raiford, and even though I had never touched any drugs there, we knew each other. I was half out of my mind when I reached his house and he fixed me up good enough to complete the whole trip. I don't know what he gave me, but whatever it was, it was beautiful. I didn't remember any of the bad things.

I have only little splashes of memory about what happened over the next ten days. I remember going to Jackie Brown's house, Allie's brother, and trying to talk to him. I remember a terrible fight. I remember a mad dash up the Georgia freeway. I remember sitting in my mother's house in Knoxville and having a violent argument. I remember leaving a Cadillac, with a signed title, with my mother. I remember getting my first tattoo. I remember writing some letters, one to Jim Russ and one to J. Edgar Hoover. I ended the letter to Russ, a mad, hysterical letter cursing him brutally, with a picture of a fox inside a crude outline of the state of Florida. Then I signed, "The Florida Fox." I have no idea where the name came from, or even what it meant, but that's the day I got the nickname that stayed with me all these years.

When I started remembering who I was, it seemed like I was walking out of a fog. I woke up lying on the most beautiful beach in the world. Next to me was a little bag. I looked inside and discovered a return airline ticket to New Orleans and less than one hundred dollars. I didn't know where any of it came from.

A few minutes later an elderly man walked over to me and asked, "Are you all right? You've been acting real strange for the last few days."

I stared at him. "Where am I?" I managed to ask.

"You're on Doctor's Cove Beach in Montego Bay, Jamaica. Can I help you?"

For the next few days he helped me an incredible amount. He was a retired factory executive from Akron, Ohio, a nice, gentle, lonely man. After all the people I had been dealing with for so long, it was wonderful to find somebody who was willing to help another human being just because it was the right thing to do.

Over the next week I started putting the pieces together as best as I could. It didn't take me long to realize I had jumped bond. I really didn't know what to do. Go back and face even more charges? Run? A life as a fugitive? There just didn't seem to be any answers.

When my money ran out I went back to New Orleans. From there

I called my father in Knoxville and his secretary told me he was in Gadsden, Alabama, on a civil engineering job. I took my last few dollars and bought a bus ticket there.

When my father opened the door of his hotel room and saw me standing there, he almost fainted. "My God," he says. "What have you done? Where have you been?"

After we settled down he asked, "Don't you know that everybody is after you? The Orlando police, the Florida police, the FBI?"

"What does the FBI want with me?" I knew I was wanted, but I didn't realize I was *that* wanted.

"They say you robbed a liquor store and pistol whipped someone."

I didn't say anything for a few seconds. "Jesus. I don't know whether I did it or not. I swear, I don't have any memory of it at all." I told him the whole story about June, the kids, and the drugs. "I just don't know."

My father, a man who believed in God, country, and the white Protestant race, had the answer. "Son, you better give yourself up. You don't have a choice."

I certainly did have a choice. "I can't do that, Pop. I just can't go back to all that shit. You don't know what they did to me down there. I can't handle it any more."

My father took me out for a nice dinner and tried to talk me into going back and trying to work through the legal system. I explained that everything was stacked against me, there was a big anti-corruption campaign going on in Orlando, and I was an ex-cop gone bad. I don't think my father understood what I was talking about, but he knew I had made my own decision.

After dinner we went walking down an alley and, right in the middle, we stopped. He pulled out his wallet and handed me a fistful of money. And then, for the first time in my thirty-one years, he put his arms around me and started crying. "I love you, son," he said.

I started crying too, and we just stood in that alley holding each other, crying and repeating over and over how much we loved each other.

That was the last time I saw my father. I had made my choice.

4 Being a fugitive is the most lonely existence in the world. I didn't dare contact my wife or any of my friends in Orlando. I had no destination, no purpose, no future, and, as far as anyone else was concerned, absolutely no past. As long as I was on the run, Jack Clouser simply did not exist.

After I had more experience, and learned the ways of the road, things did get better. But at the beginning, I simply didn't know what to do. I didn't know how to make money, how to travel, where to stay, what sort of identification to use, what stories to make up, how to pick out a cop, or even how far you can go with a good bluff and a smile.

I knew I couldn't stay in Gadsden. Orlando was totally out of the question. Knoxville was a possibility, but I still remembered the argument I had had with my mother.

Then the wildest idea came to me. The Sheik had told me about a friend of his, a big shot in the Communist party in the United States, up in New York City. I'll go to New York, I thought, and see this man. I'll get him to put me up, and then I'll wait until the Sheik gets out and we'll go to Cuba and I'll do the trip for real! I'll do it on my own, and when I get back I'll go to the Central Intelligence Agency rather than the FBI. They'll appreciate my help.

I took a bus to New York City and contacted this man through the office of the Communist paper, the *Daily Worker*. "I'm a friend of the Sheik," I told him. "I have a matter of importance to discuss with you. May I come to your place?"

"Certainly." He gave me the address and we made an appointment for that night. "By the way, what did you say your name was?"

"Frank Fox," I lied. I was getting good at it.

I showed up at his place and laid the story on him. I told him I had just gotten out of prison and I was waiting for the Sheik to get out and then we were going to go to Cuba together. I explained we were going to go to guerrilla school and learn how to cause havoc.

I never finished the story. This man jumped ten feet into the air and started screaming, "How dare you come to me with such a proposal? I don't know you. You could be anybody. Get out of here!" He literally shoved me out the door.

I was crushed. I didn't know what to do. I was in the middle of a city I'd never been near in my life, with almost no money in my pocket and no place to turn for help. All I had was a very nice jacket and a nice suitcase. I decided to try to parlay that into a room.

I went downtown and shoplifted a straw panama hat, went to the bus station and shaved, and then walked into one of the nicer hotels in midtown Manhattan. In the biggest New Orleans accent I could muster I announced, "I'm agoin' to be in this town for a couple o' weeks. I'd kinda like to stay here. How much y'all get?"

The clerk told me and I agreed it sounded like a fair price. I registered under the name of Andrew L. Jackson and then started reaching into my almost empty pocket.

"Y'all want me to pay now or—"

The clerk said I could certainly settle my bill when I checked out.

I allowed that was mighty fine of the establishment. "Nice place y'all got here, boy, very nice."

My room was big and had a terrific view. It also had a big television set and a vibrating double bed and a vibrating chair. It cost more a day than I could have afforded even if I did have any money.

New York was too much for me. I spent all my time either lying in the hotel room sleeping or wandering around the city trying to scrounge up free meals. I was successful about once a day and finally realized I had to get out of the city. This place is a jungle, I thought, I can't survive here. But I couldn't get out of town without more money.

I went to Woolworth's and shoplifted a screwdriver. Then I returned to my hotel room and pried open the coin box on the vibrating chair. Out came more quarters than I had ever seen. I put on two pairs of pants and two shirts, stuffed all my pockets full of quarters, and walked out, leaving my suitcase and the rest of my clothes in the room. The fact that I was stealing never even occurred to me, I was so desperate.

The first thing I did with my quarters was buy a big meal. Then I bought a bus ticket to Philadelphia. The only reason I picked that city was because it was as far as my money would take me. When you're on the run that is as good a way to pick a destination as any other.

Philadelphia was awful. I walked around town for thirty minutes and knew I had to get out of there. So I walked to a highway and stuck out my thumb. A trucker picked me up and took me to Baltimore. Somehow, inevitably, I was being drawn back to the South.

When we reached Baltimore the trucker offered me $8 to help him unload his truck. After we finished he took me to the company office and introduced me to his boss. The boss handed me a twenty and said, "You did a good day's work, and we're going to have a few beers. Would you go to the store and get it?"

Twenty dollars. A small fortune. I wanted it, and the urge to steal the whole $20 and keep going was very strong. But the fact that the man trusted me prevented me from leaving. So I bought a six-pack, brought it back, gave him the change, drank a beer, took my $8, and hit the road again.

The traveling wasn't too bad. I was meeting all sorts of fascinating people of all races and religions, and I was discovering that they weren't the terrible second-class citizens I had been brought up to dislike.

Of course, some of the people were problems. I was picked up on a highway near Roanoke, Virginia. We rode silently for awhile, then the driver started making small conversation. "I'm a lawyer."

I didn't want to get into any discussions. "That's nice. I'm not anything."

"Where you been?"

"New York."

"Oh, yeah. You been down to Greenwich Village?"

"Sure." This was not the most interesting conversation I had ever been in.

"I'll bet you know all the beatniks and everybody up there."

"Well, I— Not all of them."

Then he reached over and grabbed me on the leg. "I'm a homosexual."

I took his hand off my leg. "Too bad for you."

"I've got ten dollars on me." He reached in his shirt pocket and pulled out two five-dollar bills. "If you let me blow you, I'll give you five and take you right to the freeway."

I certainly wasn't going to get involved, but that money looked very good. "O.K.," I agreed.

We kept driving until he got near the freeway. Then he made a turn and went into a small, dark residential area. He stopped the car and turned and looked at me. I didn't do anything. Then he put his hand on my leg and started leaning over.

I smashed him. Just one time. Then I pushed the door open and dragged him outside.

"Don't beat me any more," he pleaded, "don't hurt me."

"I don't want to hurt you," I told him. "All I want is those two fives and your car. And I advise you to stay up here for awhile or you might get hurt." Then I took his car and started driving.

Sometimes when I think back on those days I wonder what was going on in my head. I knew taking that car was wrong, but I just didn't care. I was a desperate man. I like to think that even then there was some decency inside me, but it didn't come out too often.

So I left him up there, this freak lawyer from Roanoke, and drove to Bristol, Virginia. Bristol is on the border between Virginia and Tennessee, the state line runs right down the middle of the street. I made sure I stayed on the Virginia side—I didn't want to cross the state line in a stolen car. Then I left the car, had a meal, and hopped on a Greyhound going to Knoxville. I needed help, and even though we'd fought not long ago, my mother was the only person I could turn to.

I didn't even have enough money to get all the way home. I had to walk and hitch the last twenty miles, finally showing up about Friday midnight. I was tired and dirty when I knocked on the door. My mother answered and, for a split second, she didn't even realize who it was. Then she started crying.

Home was wonderful. I never realized how much I missed it. My sister was there and the three of us just sat around all day and all night Saturday talking about the world, the neighbors, and my problems. My mother felt the same way my father did.

"You've got to give yourself up," she kept saying, "you've got to give yourself up. The bond company's hired a special investigator and they're looking all over for you."

"Mother," I tried to explain, "I don't know what I'm going to do. Right now I just need to eat and sleep and think. Believe me when I tell you that you don't understand what they're doing to me down there."

"I do believe you, son," she told me, "I do believe you."

Early Sunday morning I felt someone shaking my foot. I opened my eyes and I was looking down the barrel of a .357 Magnum.

"You make one move, Clouser," the man holding the gun said, "and I'll blow you up."

My mother was standing in a corner of my room, crying. "I did it to save your life! I don't want them to kill you!"

They pulled me out of bed and pushed me against the wall. After a quick search—I don't know what they thought I was hiding in my pajamas—they handcuffed my hands behind my back.

40

Then they started helping me get dressed, hindering as much as helping with their pushing and shoving. All of a sudden my sister fell onto the floor and started gagging. She was having an epileptic fit. I didn't even know she had epilepsy, nobody ever told me. She was gagging and screaming, my mother was crying, the gunman had no idea what to do, and I was handcuffed and helpless. It was just heartbreaking.

We finally got my sister calmed down and my mother explained what she had done. In order to "save my life," she called the bondsman. There was a $500 reward out for my capture and he contacted the Knoxville police. It was a Knoxville detective who woke me up.

"I did it for you," she kept saying. "You won't have to go back. We'll keep you here. I'll get a lawyer and we'll get an injunction and we'll put you in a mental institution! You'll be safe."

I shook my head in disbelief. "Mama, you don't know what you're doing to me."

Right at that moment I quit being an amateur fugitive. I had learned the hardest and the most important lesson: when you run, your family and friends cease to exist. You never go back. You never contact them. They're gone, over, finished, forgotten, done. Forever.

The bondsman and his investigator showed up at the police station a few hours later. Before any lawyer could do anything they put me in the back of a car and hightailed it out of Tennessee. As we crossed the state line the bondsman said, "Whew, that was a close one. Didn't think we were ever going to get you out of Tennessee, a celebrity like you."

"What'ya mean?" I asked him.

"Didn't you hear? Half the country's been looking for you. The FBI put you on their ten most wanted list Saturday. The posters were coming out tomorrow morning."

I had been put on the list for fleeing across interstate lines, a federal charge. They knew I'd left Florida when the letters I had mailed while I was spaced out on drugs arrived. Their postmark was New Orleans.

I was half proud and half embarrassed—proud that I made the top ten and embarrassed that I only lasted one day. I figured that had to be some sort of record for futility. I didn't even have the fun of seeing my picture on a poster. My first experience as a fugitive had been a total failure.

They put me back in Orange County jail. The charges against me were piling up. Not only did I have the original Cinema Theater and gas station robberies, now they lodged two more charges against me—armed robbery of a liquor store and extortion, threatening my wife that she better not testify against me. I didn't really understand either charge. I also really, honestly, didn't know if I was guilty.

Now I'm really scared.

I know I'm innocent of the Cinema Theater and Hurricane Gas Station jobs. But I do remember seeing Allie Brown's brother, who was charged as a co-defendant in the liquor store case, and I do remember a fight. And the money and the Cadillac and the airline tickets, they had to come from somewhere. I can see I may have done the liquor store, and I'm really upset about it. I spent just about all my waking hours trying to remember something that would help me.

Jail was livable. The word had gotten around that I'd made the top ten and everyone treated me like a star. I didn't have to do any chores, I got my food first, and when I told somebody to shut up, he shut up quick, without any argument. Only I knew that I made the list by wandering around like a stupid, rambling, incoherent jerk, and I wasn't about to spread the news. I liked being Number One, even in a cell block.

Jim Russ, the district attorney, tried me first on the Hurricane Gas Station robbery. That ended in a hung jury, a technical victory for me.

Then he tried to convict me on the extortion charge. June actually got up on the stand and testified I threatened her and that I had some stolen checks from a robbery in the house. My lawyer, a public defender, explained the substance of the case to the jury. "If you're going to convict a man for extortion every time he fights with his wife, don't bother building any more schools or hospitals, just build prisons. That's all you'll need."

The jury got his point. I was found not guilty.

Two trials, no convictions. I was beginning to feel pretty confident. Then an old friend from the police force who had a good contact in the D.A.'s office came to visit me. We sat and talked for about an hour, and he laid things out very clearly for me.

"Jack," he started, "do you know what a paranoid is?"

"Certainly."

"Do you know how to become one?"

"Well, if I give it some thought," I told him, "I guess I could, you know, act like I'm being persecuted and everything."

"You damn well better practice, Jack. The word is out. You beat Jim Russ twice and he's going to hang you to the wall. If he convicts you on either one of those armed robbery trials he's going to ask for life in prison."

All of a sudden I'm not feeling very confident. You just don't beat the establishment four straight times. I knew the law of averages was going to get me, and if I lost just once they were going to put me away for the rest of my life.

I started working very carefully on my paranoia. When I lost at cards I'd accuse the other players of stacking the deck. In cell discussions I'd make a point of saying how everyone was against me. When the prison psychiatrists examined me I made up stories about everyone in the cell block plotting against me. I told them I was always the butt of the practical jokes. I told them that I heard the whispers about me.

I tried to be very careful. I wanted to establish a basis for a psychiatric cop-out if I needed one, but I didn't want to go far enough to be committed if it looked like I could beat the charges.

One afternoon I got a message from Allie Brown's brother, my supposed co-conspirator in the liquor store robbery. "Jack," he wrote, "they come to Massachusetts and brung me back. Told me you confessed to this crime and there was no chance for me except to confess and implicate you. They offered me a deal. They wanted you. If I confessed and implicated you they would go easy with me. Please don't be mad at me."

I tore up the note and flushed it down the toilet. Now I was really worried. With Jackie Brown's confession, along with some statements June made against me during the extortion trial, I had to figure it was a matter of time. I decided to go for the nut house.

I didn't figure to stay there long. Russ would be up for reelection in ten months and hopefully there would be a new district attorney. And ten months in a mental institution away from all the pressure sounded very inviting.

I started planning my mental breakdown.

In one of the books I had borrowed from the prison library I discovered a creature named Wolfram, the German god of the Black Forest. I decided that's who I would become.

My cellmate at the time was a good old country boy named Henry Sutton and nicknamed "Willie" Sutton, after the bank robber. I told him my plan and he agreed to help me out. I would sit in the corner of my cell, play the radio as loud as it would go, and howl and howl. I called it my crazy practice.

My other cellmates, who also knew what I was doing, thought my act was terrific. They would sit on the bed and give me suggestions on how to be crazy. "Willie" Sutton would shake his head from side to side and laugh. "Now roll your eyes a little, Jack, you're too sane." We had a happy time getting my act in shape.

Finally it was time for my one and only performance, the morning my retrial for the Cinema Theater robbery was scheduled to begin. I was ready. In fact, I was so ready even I was half believing I *was* Wolfram. I sent a note to my friends in the next cell telling them I would not speak to anyone after 8 A.M. At 8:30 Sutton took out the toothpaste and started painting designs all over my face. When he finished he laughed and shook my hand.

"Good luck, Jack," he said. "I hope things work out for you."

I took off all my clothes with the exception of my undershorts, sat in the corner of my cell, and let loose with one long, wonderful howl.

One of the guards came running over. "Hey, man," he said, "knock off that howling. What's the matter with you? You crazy?" Then he answered his own question. "Listen, you ain't crazy, so knock it off!"

"I'm Wolfram of the Black Forest. Aaaarrrrrooooowwww . . ." My cellmates were doing their very best to hold back their laughter.

The guard returned with a deputy. "Come on, Jack," the deputy said, "come off that goddamn faking. There's nothing wrong with you. Put your clothes on, you got to be in court in five minutes."

"Aaaaarrrrrrooooooooooooowwwwwwww!" I started slobbering all over and tried to remember to keep rolling my eyeballs like Sutton told me.

"He's nuts," the deputy finally said. "Let's get him to the head shrinkers."

Three deputies came into my cell and dressed me as I sat passively, howling only occasionally. Then they helped me to my feet and started dragging me out to the hospital. As I left I grabbed a quick peek back at Sutton. He was laughing and laughing. "There goes good old Jack," he said to no one in particular, "howling his way out of prison." I turned and howled good-bye.

I kept my act up all the way to the hospital. I could hear one of the deputies explaining to the nurse, "That's Jack Clouser, the one that robbed the Cinema Theater," but I continued being Wolfram. They decided to put me in a Florida sanitarium for forty-eight hours' observation.

Wolfram continued. I wouldn't use any utensils, I'd just scoop up my food with my hands. But slowly I began mumbling a few words. Then a few more words and not so many howls. Gradually Wolfram disappeared and I started talking again. The god of the Black Forest was gone forever, but he had served admirably.

I convinced the psychiatrists I was an extreme paranoid. "Everybody is against me," I told them. "My mother turned me in. My wife testified against me. My friends confess to lies about me."

The doctors finally went in front of the judge and said I was mentally incompetent to stand trial. I would have to be put away.

All that was left was one last trip to court to be officially declared nuts. Two deputies took me in, one handcuffed to each of my hands. As we walked in the door I spotted my bitter enemy, Jim Russ. I knew he was there to protest that I was faking. I made a split-second decision; this was going to be the frosting on the cake, my final act as a madman. I went right at him, spit right in his face, and started kicking at him. Unfortunately, I missed. I was screaming and hollering at him, "I'll live to drink your blood!"

He just stood there, rigid, shaking. The deputies twisted both my arms hard and threw me onto the floor. That was really painful and the howling I did wasn't fake for once.

Russ didn't know what to do. "This man's faking, Your Honor," he pleaded before the judge. "He's trying to avoid trial. You know it and I know it."

The judge let Russ make his statement. Then he paid no attention to it. "Jack W. Clouser, this court finds that you are mentally incompetent and unable to stand trial at this time. We sentence you to an indefinite stay at the Florida State Mental Hospital at Chattahoochee until you are able to stand trial."

As they dragged me out of the courtroom I looked toward Russ and winked my eye. I don't know if he saw me or not.

I was really happy. I had taken a long shot and won big. Wolfram, god of the Black Forest, comes to Florida. It was almost hysterical, if it wasn't so damn serious.

Ed Stock, a deputy I knew from my days in judo class, was assigned to drive me to Chattahoochee. We drove a little while and I asked, "Hey, Ed, am I legally insane now?"

He said, "Yeah, Jack, you sure are."

"Well, man, that's great. That means I can talk now." And we did talk, for more than two hours.

At one point in our conversation he warned me to keep quiet. "You know you're not crazy."

"I'm crazy like a fox," I joked, "the Florida Fox!"

He laughed too.

"No, I know I'm not crazy and you know it. But the doctors and the judge say I am, and maybe they know better than we do."

"I'd be careful what I said if I were you," he told me. "You know we got to report everything you say when we get back."

"I don't give a damn. Tell Russ. Rub it in on him that I beat him. He can't touch me now!"

It wasn't until I reached the admissions building at Chattahoochee that I realized what a stupid thing I had done. What if Russ wrote a letter or called up here? They would come right up and take me back. Everything would be undone.

Pretty quickly I had more pressing problems. After registering me into the hospital they put me in the absolute psycho maximum-security ward. This was the deep freeze for hopeless fruitcakes. There were only fifteen people in there and it was patrolled twenty-four hours a day by interns. It didn't take me long to realize that if I stayed there much longer I'd go crazy. The thought of it was funny, going crazy in the insane asylum, but the reality was terrifying. I knew I had to get out of there.

The only treatment given to people in maximum security was librium and thorazine. There was no cure and the doctors just wanted to keep the inmates as quiet as possible. Librium is just a tranquilizer, but thorazine makes you sleep sixteen to eighteen hours a day. It turned people into vegetables, doing absolutely nothing but eating and sleeping all day. I tried to palm my pills, keeping them under my tongue and throwing them down the toilet later, and most of the time I was successful. But whenever I was awake I was figuring a way out of max and into the regular looney population.

The fifth day I was there a handsome boy about twenty years old came up to me. "My name is Reggie," he said, "and I'm trying to kill myself."

I looked at him and saw he wasn't kidding. There must have been thirty healed cuts all up and down both arms. "I don't think I can help you, son," I told him gently.

46

"You got to help me die," he pleaded. "I just can't live like this."

I didn't know what to tell him. "Let me think about it," I finally said. "Maybe I can figure out something for you tomorrow."

I did think about it all night. I understood what the boy was talking about. If I knew I had to stay in max for the rest of my life I'd want to kill myself too. But I couldn't bring myself to help him commit suicide. It just wasn't right.

Finally I came up with a plan that would help both of us.

"You see that old man over there?" I asked him the next day. I pointed to a man in his mid-sixties. "You see his glasses?"

He did.

"Tonight when he goes to sleep you go over there and take his glasses. Then you bust out a lens and cut your wrist and you can die."

He was really excited. "Oh, wow! Why didn't I think of that? You're sensational." The boy was almost hysterically happy.

I had absolutely no intention of letting him commit suicide, but there was one very big danger in my plan. I had to stay awake and watch him all night. I couldn't let them force the thorazine down my throat. If I did, that boy would die.

"Here's your dinner," the aide said as he handed me my pills later that evening. "Open up!"

"I'll do it myself," I told him, grabbing the pills out of his hand. I slipped them into my mouth and under my tongue, faking a swallow.

"Open up," he said again. I did, and he inspected to make sure the pills were gone. If his eyes were better that boy would have died that night.

He missed the pills. As soon as he left I got rid of them.

Reggie followed my instructions perfectly. When the old man went to sleep the kid went over and popped out the lens. He put it on the floor and stepped on it. Then he bent down and selected one piece and began cutting into his wrist. This was one of the most fascinating things I had ever seen. I just laid there and watched, until a slow stream of blood began trickling out.

I leaped out of bed and grabbed my pillow. As quickly as I could I ripped the pillowcase right off the pillow and tore it into two large pieces. I wrapped one of them tightly around his arm, trying to stop the flow of blood.

Then I started screaming. "Hey! This man's cut himself bad! We need help! Come on, get in here!"

Help was there in seconds. I didn't like being confined but I was amazed how well Chattahoochee was run. Everything was top flight and professional, from the doctors to the janitors to the food.

Naturally a report on the incident had to be made. The report explained that inmate John Clouser acted very fast, very rationally, and administered competent first aid to the boy in an entirely sane manner. In forty-eight hours I was out of the madhouse and into the wards. The boy survived, again.

In the two years and fifty days I spent in the Florida prison system, the wards were easily the best place I stayed. It was more like a hotel than a jail. There were nurses wandering around talking freely to patients all day, television sets to watch, candy, newspapers, constant card games, and even an outdoor area for exercise. It had to be the best residence within the entire Florida penal system.

I missed my boys terribly, but I got along there very well. I managed to make really good friends with three male interns and one very cute nurse. The nurse and I became very close. In fact, we found a little room and we'd lock ourselves in for twenty minutes at the longest, but we accomplished enough in twenty minutes for both of us to be happy.

I really liked Chattahoochee. I had free time, good male companionship, one good female companion, plenty of food, and some pretty good card-playing friends. I would have been more than happy to stay inside and wait out Jim Russ. The thought of escaping never entered my mind.

Then Jim Russ's letter arrived. My plans changed. I was going to have to become a fugitive again.

5 "Sit down, Jack, let me read you this letter," Dr. David Jacobs said. "It's from Jim Russ and he says, 'We are absolutely positive that this man is faking insanity to beat armed robbery charges. We would like him judged legally sane and sent back to Orlando at the earliest convenience.' " He put the letter down and looked at me. "Is it true?"

I had been worried about this letter since the moment I arrived at Chattahoochee. In fact, I had carefully worked to convince the staff that I needed continued hospitalization, and the person I worked hardest on was Dr. Jacobs. I had heard that he was a Jewish doctor who escaped the Nazis in Europe, so the first time the orderly tried to take me to his office I threw a full-scale fit. "You're not taking me to any Jewish doctor," I screamed. "They should throw him in the ovens with the rest of them!" It was really nasty of me. Dr. Jacobs was a kind, gentle, extremely bright man, and deep inside I was embarrassed by my behavior. But I needed to make him believe I was at least a little bit crazy.

"Is it true?" he asked me again. "Are you faking?"

"I'll be really honest with you, Dr. Jacobs," I finally answered. "I just don't know. I know that I'd like to stay here for the rest of the year, that's for sure."

Dr. Jacobs sat silently, rolling his pencil on his desk for a few minutes. "Jack, I don't know what to do with you, whether to classify you as a neurotic or a psychotic. You're really a problem, you know."

"I know," I agreed, and I began getting uneasy. A psychotic is potentially a very dangerous person. If he classified me psychotic it might not be so easy to get out in ten months. I liked Chattahoochee, but I wasn't crazy about the idea of a long-term visit.

"Well," he sighed, "I guess we'll have to put you down as psychotic."

I don't know why he did it. We'd only talked a total of ten minutes and the discussion was very general. Either he believed I was psychotic because of the crimes I was accused of committing, or he was trying to back up his colleagues in Orlando, or he was trying to do me a favor by keeping me there. Whatever his reasons, when I walked out of his office I knew I didn't have to worry about staying there ten months. From his attitude I was going to be there a hell of a lot longer.

I really didn't have any options, I had to break out of the hospital.

I didn't figure I could do it alone, so I started looking around for people to take with me. I didn't have a whole lot of talent to choose from.

The wards at Chattahoochee were filled with a strange mix of inmates. There were two basic groups, the criminally insane and the civil insane. The criminals were committed by the state, the civilians by their families. Some of my fellow inmates were completely bonkers, some slightly so, and others, like myself, were faking insanity for a variety of reasons.

It wasn't too difficult to tell who was for real. We had our Napoleons, kings, dictators, movie stars, one Batman, and one Mickey Mantle. But my favorite of them all was "The Germ." The Germ was a little baldheaded guy with a big nose who believed that he would die if he breathed human air, the germs would kill him dead on the spot. So he wore a gauze mask over his mouth at all times, day and night. He was rational, sometimes funny, and mannerly, but he simply knew the germs were going to kill him.

I normally stayed away from the crazies and associated with people who were in there beating raps. It was from this group that I picked the three men to escape with me.

My first choice was one Carl Spasser, who claimed to be a hotrod expert. He swore he could start and drive any make car on the road, even without keys. Chattahoochee is set in a quiet, beautiful area covered with swamps. It's almost impossible to walk out of the area alive, therefore transportation was essential. Carl Spasser was our transportation expert.

Billy Joe Anderson was the number two man. Young Billy Joe prided himself in being the toughest man in the ward. When I arrived and he heard I was a judo expert he challenged me. "Can you break my arm with one judo smack?"

I shrugged. "I probably could."

He grabbed hold of a railing and kept his arms very straight. "I don't believe it," he said. "Go ahead, hit my arm as hard as you can."

I was laughing. "You sure you want me to do this? You're not going to be mad at me?"

"I ain't gonna be mad! Now just go ahead and hit me."

"O.K." Wham! I came down on him at three-quarter strength. I don't think I cracked the bone but I did give him a really bad bruise. For the next week, every moment I saw him he was rubbing his arm.

50

But from that point on, he was my man. He'd do whatever I told him, and as long as I made my instructions clear, he'd do it well.

My third man was Vernon Thomas, and he was in on an attempted rape charge. Vernon was a very intelligent, sophisticated person. The thing I remember best about him was that he constantly had an unlit pipe in his mouth. He really didn't have anything to contribute to the escape, but he was a nice guy and he wanted to go and I didn't want to leave him there.

That was our foursome, brains and brawn. None of them seemed real crazy to me, even though we were escaping from a mental institution. Now all we had to do was figure out a way to escape.

It was obvious to me we needed either a gun or a key. I didn't like the idea of using guns, it was important to me that no one got hurt, so that meant getting a key. I pleaded with the staff people I was friendly with and one of them finally came through. To protect this person's identity I won't divulge any information concerning how or where the key was obtained.

It was not a regular door key. There were a few notches in it, but in no way did it resemble the regular keys used to open and lock the ward doors. I was really disappointed when I got it, and I was pretty positive I could never get it to work. But to keep the morale of my little squad up I showed them the key and told them I was working on it.

And I was. I found a piece of concrete out in the yard and I just started scraping and scratching. At night I'd hide under my covers and file away at it with the clip on the end of a fingernail file. Every day, when I was positive no one was looking, I'd slip the key in a door and try to turn it. For almost two weeks nothing happened.

The key was only part of my plan. Part two was based on gaining the confidence of the interns who kept watch at night. So, while I was filing away during the day, at night I was sitting in the hall teaching Spanish to my three companions, always within eyesight and earshot of the interns.

I wanted to break out on March 29, 1964, my thirty-second birthday. But that day came and went by. The key simply wouldn't work and we couldn't get another one.

Finally, the afternoon of April 1, my fiftieth day at Chattahoochee, I put the key in the door and tried it. Click! I had to push, but it turned. The door opened! I was ecstatic, but I did my best not to show my emotion. I just slipped the key back into my pocket and went on my happy way. One by one I found my traveling companions and whispered, "It's ready. We go tonight."

For my plan to go right we needed just a little more help. The way the ward was set up, two parallel halls extended from either end of the sleeping area into a lobby. At night, one intern sat at the end of each hall, watching what was going on. We had to get the intern watching our hall into the second hall, where he couldn't see the lobby doors.

One of my other contacts on the staff had given me two hacksaw blades and I had carefully taped them under one of the other inmates' beds. There were two other men in there that I knew were desperate to escape. So I took them aside and said, "Look, I know you guys want to get out. I'll tell you what I'm going to do. I'm going to give you two hacksaw blades that will help you saw your way out, but you got to earn them."

"What do you want? Anything!"

"It's easy. At exactly eight o'clock tonight, at the far end of the hall, I want you guys to start a fight and keep it up for as long as you can before the interns break it up. O.K.?" They agreed, and I told them the blades were taped under the bed. Everything was set.

Vernon Thomas, Billy Joe Anderson, Carl Spasser, and ole Jack Clouser were busy studying their Spanish numbers at exactly eight o'clock when a fight broke out in the hallway. The intern jumped up and ran down the other hall to help the other intern break it up.

"Let's go," I whispered, and we made for the door. I whipped the key out of my pocket and pushed it into the door. It turned and the door opened. Out we go, carefully shutting the door behind us.

We went through a small area to a second door, the door guarding the stairway down to the first floor. Again the key opened it easily. We ran down the stairs.

We reached the third door, the door between the first floor and the outer lobby, without being spotted.

"Once more, baby," I said to the key as I put it in the door and turned it. The door opened, and the key broke off, right in the goddam fucking no-good lock! We had no choice but to just keep going, and pray we could make our break without needing that rotten homemade key any more.

We scrambled down the last, short flight of stairs. Now there was only one set of glass doors left between the four of us and freedom. That was exactly what Billy Joe was along for.

"Last door coming up," I whispered urgently to Billy Joe. "If it's locked you're gonna run your body through it."

He smiled happily. I was beginning to believe that maybe he *was* nuts.

Luckily, the door was wide open. Not one problem getting through. We stayed low, as much in the shadows of the building as possible, and went toward the parking lot. By now the fight on the ward had been broken up, but if we were really lucky they wouldn't realize we were gone until bed check. I had been careful to close all the doors behind us and I didn't think anyone, patient or staff, saw us get out. If they didn't miss us immediately we could count on at least a two-hour head start.

Spasser picked out a car right away and went to work under the hood with cellophane and wire. The car started right up. We all hopped in, Spasser driving, and started to make our getaway.

Freedom! I couldn't believe we'd made it so easily. I had never even thought I could pull off something like an escape from a tightly guarded institution. I wasn't really a con, I had no experience in that sort of thing. But I had done it. I'd worked out a manageable plan, picked my group, and we made it work. Now all that was between us and freedom forever were some dark, backwoods, Florida roads. I turned and watched as the lights of the main building at Chattahoochee started to disappear behind us.

All of a sudden they stopped disappearing. The car engine quit and we rolled to a dead stop.

"What's the matter?" I almost screamed at Spasser.

"Goddamned if I know," he answered as he jumped out of the car and lifted the front hood. We were about five hundred yards outside the grounds, close enough to be seen by anyone looking out a window.

"O.K.," Spasser said as he got back in the car and tried to start it. The engine caught, coughed, then died again.

"Forget it," I told him, and started getting out of the car.

"I'll fix it," he said.

I looked right at him. "I said, forget it." I turned to Billy Joe and Vernon in the back seat. "C'mon, let's get out of here."

Both rear doors opened and they climbed out.

"How?" Billy Joe asked.

"I guess we're gonna walk," I replied. Now my temper was getting short. "Unless you figure a way we can fly out."

"We gonna walk through these swamps?"

"They're the only swamps we got right now," I said as calmly as I could, and turned and walked off the road. I didn't even care who was following me, I was that pissed. The escape had gone perfectly. Perfectly! And we get stuck with a car expert who can't get a car started! What else should I expect to find in a mental institution?

It was pitch-black out, and once we got over the small hill and out of sight of the institution and its outside lights, we couldn't see a thing. We just started stumbling as far away from Chattahoochee as we could get. These were not movie-type swamps with alligators and crocodiles, they were more marshy. There would be a wet spot, then it would be dry for a quarter mile, then it would get all swampy and gooey again.

I knew that we'd never make it out if we had to walk the whole way. We had to be completely out of the area by sunrise. We had to have a car.

We kept moving forward, the four of us, always moving. Don't stop. Walk, run, trip, get up, keep moving, listen for the sirens. Dogs? So far we were about an hour into the escape and it didn't sound like we had been discovered.

Two thoughts kept running through my mind, two thoughts that you can't imagine until you've experienced them. The first was total and complete freedom. We were running wild in the woods and water, but we were free! I didn't mind falling down or running into trees, being covered with mud and grime. I was so elated to be free at last and have a fighting chance to make it.

The second thought was sadness. If you make it, I thought to myself, you'll never see your sons again. It's just totally good-bye to your whole family, everybody you love. They're lost forever.

We kept running. When one of us fell, others would pull him along until he could regain his balance. We couldn't stop. And then we saw one light in a lonely farmhouse.

We stopped. Sitting out in front of the house was a battered truck, old and dented and getting rusty. It was one of the most beautiful sights I'd ever seen.

"What about that one?" I asked Spasser. "Think you can start it?"

"No problem," he said as cool as he could.

"Yeah," I laughed, remembering what happened about an hour earlier. But we had to try it. "Vernon," I ordered, "you and Billy Joe stay here and let Carl and me see if we can get it going. When you hear the engine pop you guys make a dash and get into the back. Understand?"

"Yeah."

"O.K., Carl boy, let's go."

We started moving toward the truck, bending low and keeping the truck between us and the farmhouse so we couldn't be seen. The truck was about twenty yards away from us when we came out of the swamps. We were about ten yards away when I heard the front door open.

"I don't know who you are," a loud voice boomed, "but if you come near my truck I'm gonna blast you."

We didn't even slow down, we just turned around and went diving back into the blackness. I caught one look at the man as we took off. He was just standing there easily, holding a shotgun in both hands. I didn't doubt for one minute that he'd use it to save his truck.

Move. Move. Move. Now we were hopelessly lost. For all I knew we were moving in circles and might even wander back to the hospital grounds without knowing it.

Then the sirens started blasting. They had discovered us missing. A few minutes later we could hear the dogs. I didn't know whether they were sheriff's dogs or neighbor dogs, but they were on our trail. Now I knew I had failed, it was only a matter of time until they outran us. We had no choice but to keep moving, maybe even a little faster.

Finally one of those little miracles that you pray for all your life happened. We stumbled onto a high, dry spot, almost an island with a roadway on it. And there, sitting in the middle of the road, was an automobile.

We just couldn't believe it. In this desolate, isolated place we actually found a car. I didn't even ask Spasser if he could start it. Either he did or we went back in chains. And the dogs were getting closer.

"Here's what I want you to do," I whispered in a firm, low voice. "Vernon, you and Carl creep up low on the left side, me and Billy'll take the right. Stay down, dammit, and when you get all four doors covered I'll holler, 'Now,' and everybody jump up and yank your door open. Whoever's in there, we'll just have to grab them."

"What if the doors are locked?" Billy Joe asked. "Then whatta we do?"

"Just smash the window in with your elbow. Everybody got it?"

I raised my right arm and gave the signal. As we were crawling along the dirt I did my best to tune out the howling dogs and blasting sirens and whistles. We crawled along almost silently and, as I got closer, I could see the windows of the car were heavily fogged over.

After I got set next to the rear door on the passenger side I peeked underneath to make sure Thomas and Spasser were in position. Then I screamed, "Now!" as I leaped up and in one swift motion almost ripped the door off.

A woman started screaming; then she stopped quickly. Lying sprawled across the rear seat, half on top of the woman, was an orderly I knew from the hospital. "For God's sake," he started to say, "what the—"

I interrupted him. "Hi, Harvey, strange meeting you here."

"Jack Clouser! What the hell are you doing out here this time of night?" He certainly regained his composure pretty quickly. The girl with him turned out to be a nurse from the hospital that none of us knew. She was pretty cute, and absolutely terrified.

I didn't help calm her down. I knew we needed these people under our control. "We've escaped, you know, just a little while ago."

"That's what the sirens were all about, huh?"

"I guess. Now, Harvey, we're armed and I promise that if you do exactly what you're told you will not get hurt. We won't harm you."

Here's where taking Vernon Thomas along paid off. We didn't have a single weapon with us, but Vernon crawled into the back seat, put his hand in his pocket, and shoved the end of his pipe into Harvey's ribs.

"This is a gun," he said in a level voice. "I don't want to have to use it, but we're desperate men. Do what you're told and you won't be shot."

"Anything you tell us we're gonna do," Harvey said. "Right, honey?"

Honey agreed.

"O.K., Harvey, get out of the car," I told him.

He did and we exchanged clothes.

"Gimme your wallet."

Jackpot! He had $120 in the wallet, enough to get us well clear of Florida.

"Now get back in the back seat."

And he did exactly that.

We took off hightailing it down that highway road. Carl Spasser had been right about his driving ability. He really made that car move, and he had us in Georgia almost right away.

"Where we going?" Spasser asked.

"Atlanta," I said firmly.

Vernon Thomas spoke up. "Atlanta? What the hell are we going to do in Atlanta?"

I turned on him. "Get some money and some clothes. I have some friends there who are gonna help us. I planned this whole thing, didn't I? I got us out of there, didn't I? Believe me when I tell you Atlanta is the safest place for us to go." Then I turned around and didn't say another word.

Carl kept us moving along, speeding on the deserted roads, slowing down in the towns. Going through one of the small towns, we were stopped at a light when a local police car pulled up right next to us. The driver looked into our car and just kept looking. Shit, I'm thinking to myself, what's he looking at?

The light changed and Spasser accelerated slowly. The cop car stayed with us. I saw Carl grab a quick glance at the car and I hoped he didn't scare easily. We reached the town's second and only other light and stopped again. The police car pulled up alongside.

"Hey, buddy," the cop shouted at me.

In the back seat Vernon Thomas pushed our "gun," his pipe, into Harvey's ribs. Harvey didn't make the slightest sound.

"Yes, officer?" I asked politely.

"Your door is open," he told me, and he pointed at my door.

I looked down, and smiled. "Oh. Yes, it is." I opened it up and slammed it hard. "Thank you very much."

He nodded and the police car pulled away.

Spasser was sweating. "Jesus, I almost tore off," he said. "He really shook me."

"Well, just cool it now. Drive slow, be easy. You saw how easily I talked to him. Let's just get to Atlanta and we'll have it made."

"Oboy," Billy Joe said in the back seat, "Atlanta, here we come."

Harvey and his nurse said absolutely nothing.

My mind was working really fast now, considering all the possible options. The minute we hit that swamp I started thinking like a fugitive. With the knowledge I had gained from my first time on the run, and the additional time I had spent analyzing the mistakes I made, I had a pretty clear picture of what I had to do to stay free. The first thing was to get free of everything and everybody who knew me as Jack Clouser.

We kept driving, picking up speed and distance as we went deeper into Georgia and the dark night. Nobody said a word in the car for a very long time, then Billy Joe leaned forward and asked me in a loud whisper, "Why don't we, uh, ball this chick. Be no problem."

I had been afraid that exact topic might come up, and I knew the trouble it could cause. So I really put my foot down.

"Don't be a jerk," I almost spat at Billy Joe. "Stealing this car is bad enough. You know what they'll do to us if we ball her? You got any idea what they do to rapists in hick towns? No way in the world we'd get back to Florida in one piece." I relaxed. "Besides, Billy Joe, when we get to Atlanta we'll get all the women we want. We don't have to force ourselves on any woman. So shut up and don't make no more suggestions like that, O.K.?"

I turned around and waited to see how he'd react. For about a minute he didn't say anything. Then he leaned back himself.

"Yeah, Jack, you're right. Whatta we need this chick for when we're gonna have all the women we want in Atlanta? Isn't that right, Vernon?"

"You're right, Billy Joe," Vernon said. He understood perfectly.

I let out a big sigh of relief. But I knew it was only a temporary situation. As long as that nurse was rubbing her body next to Billy Joe we were sitting on a burning carton of dynamite.

I knew we had to get rid of our hostages. We were safely in the Georgia hills and they couldn't do us any more good. I started looking for a likely spot to stop—something on a main road, but not too well traveled at night and not too near any other people. About four o'clock in the morning, on the crest of a Georgia hill, I found a perfect spot. "Stop the car, Carl," I said casually.

He pulled over to the side of the road. After his first failure he had done a good job for us. "What's up?" he wanted to know.

"You guys take a leak and stretch your legs and relax. I'm going to take Harvey and his nurse here and tell them what I want them to do. O.K., everybody out of the car." I waited until my partners and our hostages had climbed out, then I reached in back, grabbed the blanket, and climbed out myself. "Follow me," I ordered Harvey and the nurse.

We walked about thirty yards behind the car and stopped. "Look," I said, "I'm really sorry all of this happened, but we were desperate men. Here's a blanket. Now, why don't you guys just wrap yourselfs up over on the side there. It'll be daylight in a couple of hours. If you try to walk down the mountain in this darkness you may get in trouble, you know, fall down, anything. Just stay up here and take it easy. When daylight comes just walk on down the hill and flag a car."

"You took all our money," the nurse said.

I was a little embarrassed. "Listen, someday, in some circumstances, maybe I can make restitution. I'm really sorry." I reached in my pocket and pulled out Harvey's roll. I peeled a $10 bill off the top. "Here. I know you guys will be hungry and cold and everything. This is enough so you can buy a good breakfast and plenty of coffee. But don't tell anybody I gave this money to you. Good luck, O.K.?"

They didn't say anything. They both just stared at me. I turned and walked back toward the car.

About halfway there I stopped and bent over and picked up a handful of Georgia clay. I rubbed it in my hands and looked up to the sky. It was one of the clearest nights I'd ever seen and the heavens were just packed tight with stars from horizon to horizon. I could feel the freedom in the air. Here we go, I thought to myself, the first day of a new adventure, the first day of freedom. And then I opened my mouth and spoke out loud. I don't know where the words came from.

"If there's a God in heaven, just give me ten years of freedom and a good life"—I just picked a figure out at random, it had no real meaning—"and show me how to survive without having to steal or rob, and I swear, so help me, this is the last time I'll ever take a penny I'm not entitled to as long as I live."

I stood there for a little while longer, staring straight up, wondering if anyone was listening to me. Then I took one deep breath and started walking back to the car.

"O.K., O.K., everybody get back in," I ordered.

I was the last one inside, back in my seat next to Carl Spasser. "O.K., hotrod," I said to him, "take this heap to Montgomery."

For the first time since the break, Vernon Thomas showed some emotion.

"Montgomery!" he blurted out. "I thought you had people in Atlanta to take care of us!"

I twisted around in my seat so I could see him. "Vernon, you are now a fugitive. There are men looking all over for you. Tomorrow when Harvey and his girl friend get picked up, they're going to tell the police that us four nuts are on our way to Atlanta. So if you want to go to Atlanta you just go right ahead. But there's gonna be one hell of a welcome party waiting to meet you there. Got it?"

Billy Joe answered for him. "Damn," he said, shaking his head in admiration, "that old Jack is sure one hell of a thinker." He looked right at me. "I do admire you, Jack Clouser."

We drove through the night, crossing into Alabama. Now we'd crossed three states. I knew we were open for the federal charges of interstate transportation of a stolen vehicle, but I didn't mention it to my partners. It was an accomplished fact and I didn't want to give them anything else to think about. They were having enough problems just getting along.

The sun came up a little after six and about an hour later we pulled into the back parking lot of a beat-up diner. I knew by now every law-enforcement officer in the South was looking for four men traveling together in a black, late-model sedan. If we stayed together we didn't stand a chance of completing our getaway.

I laid it right out for them. "This is where we split up. They're looking for four men, so we got to break up and go in pairs. Now—"

"I'll go with you, Jack," Billy Joe interrupted.

"Jack, I'd like to go with you," Carl Spasser said.

I didn't want either of them. Vernon Thomas was much smarter and had the potential of really helping. "Thank you," I told them, "that's really nice. But listen, I know neither of you likes ole Vernon here"—that was true, they thought he was a drag—"and so you two go together and I'll take him with me.

"I'm gonna split up the money we took," I went on. "Vernon and me are gonna go to the Greyhound station and you two go to the Trailways station. Buy tickets to New Orleans. Don't sit together on the bus and don't ever even talk to each other. When you get to New Orleans we'll meet in the lobby of the Jung Hotel. That's pretty simple, right?"

"I think we can do that with no trouble," Carl answered.

"I know you can," I said confidently. Inside I knew they didn't stand a chance and I felt guilty about it. I had three people depending on me, like children depend on their father, to keep them safe and free. For the first time I realized that I had used these men to help *me* escape. I owed them for that, I thought. But I kept thinking, I never promised them anything except to get them free. I got them free. I fulfilled my part of the bargain. They had to survive or be captured on their own. And this was as good a time as any to set them loose.

We split up the money I took from Harvey into four equal shares of $29. Aside from that fortune I had an additional $50 I had won in small-stakes poker games on the ward rolled up tight and stuffed inside a fountain pen. That brought my life savings to a grand total of $79.

"We'll see you guys in be-you-tee-ful New Orleans," I said to Carl and Billy Joe as we shook hands. "You all be careful now."

They turned and started walking toward the Trailways station. It was the last time I ever saw either of them.

Vernon had $17 of his own money, so he was rolling in dough too. We decided to celebrate by buying brand-new wardrobes, a costly but very necessary expense. As we were walking down the streets looking for a cheap clothing store I tried to imagine what was going on in Atlanta. Cops had to be swarming all over the highways waiting for us. I knew my plan had bought us time, but how much time?

We found a secondhand clothing store and both of us bought olive-green work pants and work shirts. Vernon got a cap and I bought myself a dandy straw hat. Then we happily threw our Florida State Hospital clothes in the garbage in the back of the store and went to the Greyhound station.

"I'm going to go in first, Vernon," I told him. "When you come in don't talk to me. Pretend like you don't know me. Just wait until three or four people get in line behind me, then you get in line, and buy yourself a ticket to Nashville, Tennessee."

I knew that one was going to surprise him.

"Nashville?" he almost shouted. "Aren't we going to New Orleans to meet Billy Joe and Carl?"

"No way," I explained. "Don't you realize that the four of us aren't ever going to make it? Don't you see that?"

"Well, you're right, dammit. But Jesus, I didn't think that we would—"

I stopped him. "It's like this. If you want to go with me, then you do what I say when I say it, and if you don't, then you're on your own. Which is it?"

He didn't even stop to think. "I'll go with you."

"O.K.," I said. "Now I don't want to hear any more about the others. We're through with them. Let's get on the bus."

Bus companies are God's gift to fugitives. I discovered that fact the first time I was on the run. No one checking you, no one hassling you, no one bothering you. And you cover ground quickly.

We both got to Nashville without any problems. I knew we were far enough away from Florida to safely associate with each other. So we had a meal there, hopped on a Trailways, and went through Knoxville to Roanoke. It's always a smart idea to switch bus lines when you stop in a city. Helps keep your trail hard to follow.

I felt absolutely nothing when we drove through Knoxville, and I made no attempt to contact any of my relatives. The memory of waking up to find a gun stuck in my face was still too strong.

There was no place in the country for me to head for, no one I could safely turn to for help. I decided my best chance was to get lost in the easiest place in the world to get lost in, New York City. And I had just enough money to buy one full-fare ticket from Roanoke to New York.

Vernon had nowhere near enough. "I'm buying my ticket on Greyhound," I explained. "What do you want to do? Think you can hitchhike from here up to New York?"

He nodded.

"Good. Tell you what I'll do. There's a place in Greenwich Village called Washington Square Park that's got a big fountain right in the middle of it. Today's Tuesday. On Thursday night and Friday night, both of those nights, I'll be at the fountain at exactly eight o'clock. If you're there I'll take you with me, but if you're not there by Friday at eight-thirty then I'm taking off."

"That's O.K. with me," he said, "but can you make it Friday and Saturday nights? My mother doesn't live too far from there and I want to go visit her one last time."

I laughed out loud. "Let me tell you something, Vernon, you're making a terrible mistake. You can't go see your mother or any other family member. If you do, I promise you you're gonna be sorry. I guarantee it."

He didn't believe me. "No, Jack, it's my mother, for God's sake. My mother."

I just shrugged my shoulders. There was no way I could explain to him that he had to forget his mother, his father, his whole family, and all his friends. We were standing outside the bus station in a light rain, and there was just no way he would understand.

"Good luck, Vernon," was all I said. "I hope you make it to New York."

"Don't worry," he said emphatically, "I'll make it there."

We shook hands good-bye. And that was the last time I ever saw Vernon Thomas.

When I got on the bus and took off for New York, my escape was complete. Jim Russ, June, my mother, my father, my sister, and even Dr. Jacobs were all left behind. I had no money and no plans. I was going to follow whatever ideas I had. Although I was being chased by state and federal police, for the first time in many years I really felt like a free man.

I knew one person in New York, a former Florida bank robber named Frank Boswell that I had become friendly with in Orange County jail. When he got out he gave me his address in Yonkers and told me to find him if I ever got to the city. I didn't figure he would let me stay with him, but I hoped he'd at least loan me some money.

It turns out he wouldn't let me stay anywhere else. Boswell had a fantastic setup going for him. The apartment in Yonkers belonged to his mistress and her four children. He also had a house in Scarsdale, where he lived with his wife and three children.

I told him the whole escape story and warned him that the heat might be looking for me. He didn't care at all.

"Don't worry about it," he said. "You're safe now."

Then he proceeded to dye my hair for the first time, changing it from blond to very dark brown. When I stepped back and looked in the mirror I was amazed. I couldn't believe that something as simple as changing my hair color could make me look so different. Boswell had used disguises in his bank work, so he knew a lot about makeup, particularly hair coloring. He showed me the best kinds to use, the best times to use it, and the proper way to mix it. That was the very first disguise I used, and from that point on I had dark hair for almost a year.

Boswell also found me a way to make money. He himself was on parole in New York and had to have a legitimate job. His job, his front really, was managing a pool room. His real job was selling marijuana.

On Friday morning he took me to the pool hall. I helped him clean

As a fugitive, Clouser disguised himself by frequently changing his hair c[ol]or and style, by growing and shaving off his beard and mustache, and by gai[ning] and losing weight.

up and hung around all day and he paid me a few dollars. That night he drove me down to Washington Square and waited until I searched for Vernon. We did the same thing Saturday night. The man just wasn't there. How he was captured I don't know, but he never made it to the fountain.

On Monday I went to work for real at the pool hall. I was living at Boswell's house in Scarsdale, making money, and beginning to feel comfortable. But the fact that I was a fugitive never left my mind. I was always looking over my shoulder, picking out people and checking to see if they were following me. I would often go a few blocks out of my way, just to make sure no one was on my tail. Every time the phone rang or there was an unexpected knock on the front door I took a deep breath and figured I had been found. There was absolutely not one minute of peace. As the weeks went by, I began to realize that the longer I stayed out, the longer the odds became against me staying free. They *had* to be closing in on me.

Boswell had just about given up his pool hall job and was now dealing in grass almost all day. After a month he asked me "to go along in case somebody hassles me, you know, protect me, and carry the money." It seemed like an easy way to make good money.

And it was. Soon I made enough money to get a very small apartment of my own in the Bronx. Each morning Boswell would pick me up and we'd make rounds all over New York City, selling anywhere between $5 and $50 at each stop. It wasn't tough work.

He did a good job watching out for me. He had me fitted for a pair of glasses, which I took to wearing all the time, and convinced me to grow a mustache, which I dyed to match my hair. With the glasses, stash, and hair coloring I didn't look very much like Jack Clouser. Boswell also got me three pieces of identification with his name on them—his social security card, a library card, and a piece of wallet identification with the name typed in. "If you ever need these, you got my permission to use them," he said.

I knew it was an important start for me. "Thanks, man," I told him, "but if I do that's really gonna mess you up with the tax department."

He just laughed. "I don't pay no taxes anyway. Don't worry about it."

The cards made me feel a lot safer. Now I had something to show if I got picked up. In my own head I invented a whole life for myself using Frank Boswell's name. Where I was born, grew up, went to school, got married, kids, everything. If I did get picked up I had some quick answers ready, maybe quick enough to help me get loose.

The only thing that was missing from my life was a woman. I'd met a few in Bronx bars, but nothing to write home about even if I was writing home. I decided to try to find someone worth spending time with. That was my mistake. Women have been my downfall. I should have just left well enough alone and been satisfied. But I wasn't.

At a party one weekend I met a friend of Boswell's nicknamed Ratsy. Ratsy, it turns out, is separated from his wife and the way he talks about her it doesn't sound like there is any chance of them getting back together. He's walked out on her for about eight different reasons and he makes it sound like he hates her. Then a few days later I meet her at Boswell's house, and she is beautiful.

I was looking for a woman to play with, not marry, so later in the week I looked up her phone number in the directory and called her. I introduced myself under the phony name I was using, I don't remember what it was, and told her I'd been with her husband. "He told me that you're separated and I thought maybe you and I could get together one night and have dinner." I was very polite.

She was also very polite. "I don't know. I have hopes of getting back with my husband. I don't think I'm available."

"Fine," I said. "I hope you don't mind me calling and asking."

"No, of course not."

We hung up. It was a very polite and very short conversation. This was on a Friday.

On Monday Boswell didn't show up. It had happened before so I didn't let it bother me. On Tuesday he didn't show up. That was unusual. And again on Wednesday he didn't show up. Obviously something was wrong.

I called him up in Westchester. "Hey, man, where you been? What's going on here?"

He didn't sound very friendly. "Oh, man, how could you do what you did?"

"Do what?"

"What, shit," he said. "You called Ratsy's wife, propositioned her, said all kinds of filthy things into the phone, told her—"

I cut him short. "What are you talking about? I didn't do anything like that!"

"That's not what she says. She told my wife, and *she* told Ratsy. Ratsy is really pissed off. He begged me to tell him where you lived and I gave him a phony address. He's sitting there right now, waiting for you, with a shotgun. He's gonna kill you."

"Jesus Christ." I didn't know what to do. "Boswell, I swear, this is a bum rap. I never did anything like that. Look, let's get everybody together, you, your old lady, Ratsy, and his wife, and we'll sit down and straighten the whole thing out right now."

"Not a chance," he answered. "He's going to shoot you down on sight. My wife told him you were a fugitive and he knows if he shoots you they won't do anything to him. You better split from New York."

The way it sounded I knew he was right. Even if Ratsy didn't find me, it was possible he'd alert the police I was in the city. I didn't know which was worse, getting shot by Ratsy or being shipped back to Florida by the New York police. Leaving New York had to be better than either possibility.

"You know that I'm holding a hundred bucks of yours," I told Boswell. "You better come down here and let me give it to you."

"Forget it. Take it with you. Next time you're through, call me and I'll collect."

I hung up and I could feel the anger starting to rise again. I couldn't understand how I was in the middle again. The only person who didn't like me was Boswell's wife, who was afraid Frank would be arrested for harboring a fugitive. But set me up to be shotgunned?

It was obvious New York was finished. I had to move again, but where to go? South, I decided. Not to Florida, but close enough to pick up a newspaper and see what was happening down there. I finally decided on Myrtle Beach, South Carolina. I had no real reason except that I had heard it was a terrific place to have fun. And, when you're running, and you have no place to be at no particular time, that's as good a reason as any.

I left New York with $100 of Boswell's money, another $250 of my own, glasses, a mustache, a new hair color, and a passable set of identification. When I got to Myrtle Beach I didn't look for a job immediately. Instead I decided to lie on the beach for a few days. It didn't take me long to meet the next woman in my life. Her name was Elaine Mekler.

I would guess Elaine was about thirty-seven at this point, five years older than I was, but still passable-looking. I could see immediately that she was lonely, and I knew I was horny, so we made a perfect couple. We spent all day on the beach, then went out for dinner and finally went to her place. I've never forced myself on any woman and didn't start that night. She explained she was tired and I left and went back to the apartment I'd rented, about three blocks away. We didn't make any specific plans to get together again.

68

The next day I met a young man named Dexter Harrison. We spent the whole day talking and a good portion of the night getting drunk together. It was after one in the morning, it was now Friday, that we split up. He shouted that he would meet me on the beach the next afternoon.

He never showed up. I didn't concern myself one way or the other. He was a nice guy and we had a good time together. That was it. I spent the day lying on the beach and lining up a part-time job for myself. This was in June 1964, and the boardwalk was just opening up. I was hired to run the basketball concession on Saturdays and Sundays, starting the next day.

Friday night I went back to the bar Dexter and I got drunk in Thursday night, thinking maybe I'd run into him again. It wasn't too crowded, there were people drinking, the band was warming up, when all of a sudden I felt a tap on my shoulder. I turned around to find a big man with a big gun and a big badge. A plainclothes detective. "You want to come with me, please?"

My heart sunk right out the bottom of my feet. How the hell did they find me? Who picked me out? I had no choice but to do everything he told me to. "Certainly," I answered him, and he walked me outside.

"Do you have any identification on you?" he asked when we were alone. Carefully not making any moves he could interpret as going for a gun, I pulled out Boswell's three pieces and handed them over. He examined them very slowly, then said, "I'd like to take you downtown and ask you some questions."

"Yes, sir."

On the way to the station I decided to try the big bluff. If they didn't know who I was there was always the chance I could get free before they checked my fingerprints with the FBI in Washington.

"What do you guys want with me?" I asked in the car.

"You'll see," the plainclothes detective answered in a tired voice. I started working up a story in my own mind. I wanted to have answers prepared for every question they might ask. I figured out a whole life in the twenty minutes it took to get to their headquarters.

Their commanding officer did the questioning. "How long you been in town, Mr. Boswell?"

The fact that they were calling me Boswell made me start hoping they didn't know who they had on hand.

"Three days."

"Where do you live?"

I told him the address.

"What are you doing here?"

That's when I went into my act. I had prepared the most outland-ish, ridiculous story I could conjure up. I hoped that the cops would believe it was too silly to make up. In my best New York accent I began, "I'm a Protestant and my wife is a Catholic. She took on her priest as her lover and I just can't stand it. It's a religious thing and we fight about it every minute and there's children involved and I just had to get away. So I quit my job, got out my savings, and just took the first bus that was leaving the terminal. Here I am, trying to forget my troubles with my wife. You're not a Catholic, are you, sir?"

He wasn't, and I don't think he appreciated my asking. "You get yourself a job down here?"

I nodded my head vigorously. "I sure did. Starting tomorrow I'm managing the basketball concession on the boardwalk. You ever play basketball, sir?"

He was busy writing down everything I said. The more he asked, the more I began to believe they didn't know who I was. Whatever they were questioning me about then, it couldn't be as bad as the truth. He finally pulled open his desk drawer, took out a stack of photographs, and threw them down next to me. I picked them up and started looking at them. They were pictures of a dead body, after an autopsy, lying on a slab in the morgue, I guessed. The body was a deep, dark color and bloated. It was nobody I had ever known.

I shook my head. "Sorry, sir, I never seen this guy before."

He raised his eyebrows. "You sure?"

"Positive."

"That's funny, because the bartender at the Old Oak says you spent all night Thursday drinking with him. His name was Dexter Harrison, and it seems you were the last person anybody saw him with before he was killed."

Now I really had problems.

7

Dexter Harrison had been shot full of so many holes he looked like a pin cushion. I sifted through the pictures one by one. It was difficult to be sure it was him, but the more I looked, the less doubt I had.

"How—I mean what—where—" I couldn't believe that I had escaped into a situation like this. At that moment, Orlando's thirty years looked very inviting. "How did this happen?" I finally managed to blurt out.

"This man was shot to death at six o'clock this morning while attempting to burglarize a clothing store. The policeman that killed him believes he may have had an accomplice with him. Since you were the last person seen with him, it does whet our interest in you."

I let my deep breath out. It wasn't murder they were trying to pin on me, only a simple burglary. On the other hand, when the Myrtle Beach police got my records and discovered I was a fugitive running from two armed robbery indictments, my chances of beating this charge were very slim. My only hope was to get out of town before the cops checked my records with Washington and my story with New York.

"Listen," I told the commander, "I swear to God I left him before two o'clock. I had nothing to do with any burglary. I hardly even knew the guy. We just met." I really laid it on thick, but it was the complete truth.

We went back and forth for a few hours. Finally the commander realized I wasn't going to break and he knew he had to let me go. "Boswell," he explained, "I'm gonna turn you loose now, but I want you to stay in town and I want to see you on the job. Got it?"

"Yes, sir, yes, sir." I would have agreed to buy the Brooklyn Bridge in order to get out of his office. I walked out of the police station thinking, I've gotta get outta here, I've gotta run. But by the time I got back to my room my thinking was a little clearer. I knew the police were going to be watching me. Be cool, I thought, be cool. Don't make that break. The fact that it was the beginning of the weekend made me feel a little safer. That would slow them down and they probably wouldn't be able to check my identification until Monday. I figured I had forty-eight hours to make my getaway.

I knew Saturday was just too soon, they'd still be watching me. So I went to work and managed to get through the day. Sure enough, toward Saturday evening the commander showed up on the board-

71

walk. He just nodded and walked right by. My stomach was doing flip-flops, but I put on my most innocent smile. At the end of the day I went to my boss and asked for my salary for the day. He gave me three-quarters of it and told me he'd pay me the rest after the weekend.

The first bus leaving on Sunday morning was at seven o'clock. I guessed that Sunday was the commander's day off. He saw me Saturday, I didn't look like I was going to run, he was satisfied. If I left Sunday morning I'd have at least a twenty-four-hour head start.

The only thing that worried me was the possibility the police had alerted the bus companies to be looking out for a man fitting my general description. It would really be nice, I decided, to have a traveling companion, particularly someone to purchase the tickets. The only conceivable possibility was the woman I met on the beach, Elaine Mekler.

I went to Elaine's apartment Saturday night to invite her along. "I'm splitting," I told her. "You want to come along?"

All she asked was where I intended to go.

I hadn't even considered it. "First let's go up to Raleigh or Charleston, then decide."

"I'm really getting tired of Myrtle," she said. "I'll go with you."

"Good. I'll come by about six-thirty tomorrow morning." Then I went home and spent a sleepless night. The first thing I did the next morning was shave off my mustache and put my glasses back on. I picked Elaine up and we went downtown and got on the bus without a single problem.

I'm out of it, I thought. Jesus, I'm happy. I couldn't believe I got out of that place. If the police had done any real checking they would have put me behind bars real quick. Come Monday morning and they can't find me, they're going to be very upset. That bus couldn't move fast enough or far enough for me.

On the bus ride I started doing some thinking. I hated being on the run. Freedom was beautiful, but I really couldn't enjoy it. I was always watching my rear, always thinking, always wondering, never relaxing. I even considered going back to Orlando and shooting up all the people who were giving me problems. Get some weapons and clean out the whole crowd, then say, "Here I am, take me." I was legally insane, there was very little they could do to me. But it never went

72

beyond short thoughts. Killing was always something I hated. I just wanted to survive and be free. And I was physically free, I just couldn't seem to get free of the terrible strain of my memories.

I thought about my sons a great deal. I considered going back and trying to steal them. The only thing that kept me running was the realization that, if I did get caught, I wouldn't be the slightest bit better off. I still wouldn't have them. And I wouldn't have my freedom. I had to keep running.

"Where did you say you were from?" Elaine asked, bringing me back to reality.

I made up a tangled lie for her to try to follow. Then I figured I'd better change the subject, and started asking her questions about her life.

"I've just been released from a mental hospital," she said very casually.

Boom! That was a kicker. "Um, what were you committed for?" I asked easily.

She shrugged her shoulders. "You know," she answered.

I didn't, but I didn't want to press her. I just decided to watch her very carefully and, at the first sign of any problems, steer very clear.

We spent our first night together in Asheville, North Carolina. We made love all night, and everything was calm and wonderful. In the middle of the night we decided to go somewhere that neither of us had ever been and see what it was like. That someplace was Cleveland, Ohio. Why? I'll never know. But Cleveland, Ohio, it was.

It was during the bus ride to Cleveland that all kinds of weird things began to happen to Elaine's mind. She started talking crazy. "Frank, you know, I think I'm pregnant."

"Really?" I didn't know what else to say.

Then she said in a loud voice, "I don't want to have a baby!"

People started turning around to look at us. I whispered in her ear, "It'll be all right, honey, everything'll be fine." I wasn't too sure. Every few hours during the trip she'd start talking about the baby. Whenever she did I hugged her very tightly and did my best to keep her quiet. The one thing I didn't need was attention.

We made it into Cleveland and checked into the first decent hotel we found. No sooner had we taken our clothes off and gotten into bed than she starts moaning, "Oh, oh, my baby's coming. I'm gonna have my baby right now. Help me, please help me."

"I'm here," I said softly. "I'm here." One thing I learned at Chattahoochee is that you cannot reason with insane people. It's absolutely foolish to argue with them.

"Feel him. He's moving."

I reached over and put my hand on her stomach. "By golly, you're right," I told her. "He is just about ready to be born. You are definitely going to have a baby. I tell you what we'll do. First thing in the morning, we're gonna get up, check into a hospital, and we're gonna have our baby." That satisfied her and she dozed off into a deep sleep.

As soon as I was sure she was out I got up, put my clothes on, got my little traveling grip, and walked out the door and out of her life forever. That woman was a real fruitcake, and needed help, but I just wasn't in a position to help her. A fugitive cannot afford to associate with people who might draw attention to him.

Once again I had to start all over. I had a few dollars, no job, no place to stay, and no friends to turn to. I took care of my most immediate need, a place to stay, first. I found a fleabag hotel and checked in. Then I started walking the streets, looking for work, anything that paid American dollars. My search started and ended at a labor pool office.

"Daywork. Men only," the sign hanging in the window said. I went in and signed up, using Boswell's social security number as proof of identity. The man behind the desk never even looked up at me. "Be here at six tomorrow morning," he said in a bored voice. "We'll try to get you out on something."

A day-labor pool works as a human supply company. If a business needs a number of men to do a temporary job, they contact the labor pool and hire them on a day-by-day basis. You're paid at the end of every day you work. Best of all, nobody asks any questions about who you are or where you're from.

Next day I was there right on time. And I sat there from six until noon without being sent out to work. On Wednesday the same thing happened. My money was really getting short now and I was getting desperate, but I was afraid to say anything because I didn't want to antagonize anyone.

Finally, on Thursday, I got out. Twelve of us were loaded on a bus and driven to a mill outside Cleveland. There, for a dollar and a quarter an hour, we put on huge raincoats and steam-blasted furnaces. It was hot, dirty work, but it really felt good to be using my muscles

74

again and putting in a hard day's work. Incredible as it might seem, you can learn to miss that tired feeling you get after putting in a tough workday, if you're denied the opportunity to work.

At the end of the day they handed me ten dollars in cash. From then on I got sent out every day and got paid my ten dollars every afternoon. I was so happy to be free I would have worked for nothing more than room and board. Some of the guys, they got their ten dollars and went right next door, ate their meal, bought a jug of wine, and rented a cheap room to sleep and booze in. Not me. I saved. I didn't booze it, I didn't hit the street at night. I'd go home and go to bed five nights a week. But on Friday and Saturday I'd go into a bar, pick up some girl, and take her home. Anything to keep the old average going.

After a few months I had a pretty good reputation at the labor pool office. I showed up ready for work every day and they never got any complaints about me. Eventually they sent me to a place in West Cleveland called the Marsh Allen Company, a manufacturer of iron furniture. I worked there every single day, ten dollars a day, for less than a month. Then I was called into the foreman's office. "Boswell, we have a thing we work with the labor pool. Whenever we find exceptional workers the pool gives us permission to hire them as regular employees. Would you like to come work for us?"

"Absolutely." The fact that I had to fill out a regular job application didn't bother me. I just made up all the answers. They weren't going to check, they just wanted people who would put in a solid day's work five days a week, and I had proved that I would. That was all the information they wanted about anybody.

At first I started working a punch press, but within a few weeks I was shifted to the so-called king line, where the best workers were stationed. It was working on the king line that I made my very first Jewish and black friends. I was amazed, the Jew didn't have horns and didn't talk only about money, and neither of my black friends smelled funny or particularly liked fried chicken or watermelon. The four of us became very close friends and we started drinking and gambling and just hanging out together. I was feeling very safe and secure. I had friends, a place to stay, and an income. The only additional need I had was for a woman companion.

I went through a long list in Cleveland until I met my sweet little redheaded SueEllen Hoffman. I met her in a local bar one night, and after we both got stone-face drunk, I picked her up and carried her across the street and down the block to my apartment. I took her up to

75

my room and naturally she was protesting, it wasn't even our first date, just a pickup, but eventually she decided we should make love and we had a tremendous sexual experience. We fell in love that night. Really, honestly in love. It had never happened to me before.

Unfortunately, SueEllen had a husband. Although she was separated from him, he was incredibly jealous, and used to follow her around. He was a brute, a real animal, a slob. He would just come in whenever he wanted and take her by force.

"I hate him," she cried one night. "He thinks he can do anything he wants with me."

"Well, those days are over. You want to move in with me, I'll protect you and I'll take care of you and he won't bother you any more."

She moved right in the next day.

The summer of 1964 was coming to an end and I was very happy. I had everything I wanted, except my sons. But I knew everything was going to end a few months later. At the end of the year I was going to have to leave Cleveland because Marsh Allen was going to file tax returns with my social security number on them. And it wasn't my social security number. When the discrepancy was discovered I would be in big trouble, so I simply had to leave.

It was too bad, because by this time I had become assistant foreman in my section. I was hard working, on time, and conscientious. A perfect worker.

The only problem I had at that time, and compared to what I had been through it was absolutely nothing, was SueEllen's husband. He was looking everywhere for her, and making threats about what he would do when he found her. I wasn't scared. I was tough and figured I could probably take him, but I couldn't risk getting involved with the police. So we did our best to avoid him. We changed bars, stayed out of certain neighborhoods, and never went near his apartment or his business area.

Our luck ran out one night, though, and we saw him coming down the street. We ran up an alley and over a barbed-wire fence. I made the fence with no problem, but SueEllen cut her hand. At home we bandaged it and stopped the blood, but she just couldn't stop crying. I held her very tightly and I felt very close to her, and I made the one fatal mistake I never should have made.

"I'm not Frank Boswell," I told her. "He's just a guy I know in New York." She was the only person I ever told.

"I don't care who you are," she said, "I love you."

"I can't tell you my name, but I'm a federal fugitive."

She stopped crying completely. "I don't care, I told you. I love you and I want to be with you." So we spent the entire night holding each other. I told her my whole background and it didn't seem to bother her at all.

"I swear," I said to her, "I never did any of those things they're accusing me of."

It made absolutely no difference to her. She seemed to forget about it as soon as I told her. Because my friends were always around she continued to call me Frank, and after that night she never questioned me about my past again.

We were really happy together. SueEllen was working as a day maid and between our two salaries we were managing to save some money. Our nights were spent either by ourselves or with my Jewish and black friends. I had become very close to the three of them.

I couldn't understand how my parents could have been so prejudiced as to poison their own child's mind. And I couldn't believe that I had listened to them and actually believed them. I thought, There must have been some truth to what they tried to teach me. I really wanted them to be partially right, so I wouldn't feel I'd wasted so much of my life thinking such garbage.

In late September Barry Goldwater came to Cleveland in the middle of his campaign against Lyndon Johnson for the presidency. Now Senator Goldwater was someone who seemed to be saying many of the same things my parents taught me, and I decided to go downtown to his rally and try to reconfirm in my mind the things I had been taught.

As I walked around the last corner and started to turn left from the front entrance, my mind was on Barry Goldwater and not on protecting myself. With my dark hair growing longer, my mustache, my glasses, and the beret I had taken to wearing, I felt almost undetectable. I didn't expect to run into trouble. And that is always the time that trouble seems to happen.

There was a guy standing on the corner, leaning against the wall, just staring into space. I took one look at him and the bells started going off in my gut. No question about it, this guy was fuzz. I've got a sixth sense about danger and it was sending out heavy storm warning signals. So instead of turning left for the rally, I turned right and walked directly into a bar, sat down, and ordered a beer.

He must have had a sixth sense working too. Within a few minutes he walked into the bar and sat down on the stool next to me. "God damn Goldwater," he said into his beer.

I paid no attention. Instead I was working up a good, solid story.

You have got to always have a story ready. Always. It makes almost no difference what it is, it's got to be on the tip of your tongue and roll right off. Anybody who questions you is going to ask your social security number, your serial number in the service, your mother's maiden name, your father's name, his business, your religion, your marital situation, and your home town. A successful fugitive has the answers before the questions are asked. A good questioner will come back and ask the same question over and over: "What'd you say your mother's maiden name was?" If you don't have the same answer every time then you're in trouble. You have to drill yourself, just like in school.

This guy was being cool. Again he mumbled something nasty about Goldwater under his breath, just loud enough for me to hear. I just kept drinking my beer and staring straight ahead into the mirror. Finally he grabbed my arm and leaned in close. "You hear this one about Barry Goldwater?" Then he proceeded to tell me a dirty joke about Goldwater.

He laughed out loud. I didn't even crack a smile. "I don't think that's too funny," I said as friendly as I could. I was sweating. It was obvious this guy had no idea who I was but he was trying to feel me out. As long as I kept my cool I knew I'd be all right.

"Well," he continued, "then let me tell you about the other guy." Then he told me a similar dirty joke about Johnson.

Actually it was a pretty funny joke, but I didn't laugh. "You know," I told him, "I'm not all that interested in politics. Why do you keep talking about it?" I was casually searching his body with my eyes, looking for a holster bulge somewhere. I couldn't find it. It was possible I was wrong, that this wasn't a cop of some sort, but I just couldn't gamble. He was suspicious to begin with, otherwise he wouldn't have followed me into the bar, and I couldn't do anything to encourage his feelings.

"Lemme show you something," he then said, reaching under his jacket. I thought he was going for his gun, but he pulled out a crumpled cartoon. It was a mimeographed drawing of Johnson doing some sexually obscene contortion. "Isn't that funny?" he asked.

"No, that's not funny at all," I said honestly. "Listen, politics just isn't my game, you know?"

Right away he asks, "What is your game?"

I had my answer all ready. "My game is ladies and horses."

"Oh, you're a gambler?" He was really trying to feel me out.

I knew I had to cut the conversation short. In a loud, irritated voice I said, "I'm a gambler and I don't give a fuck about politics and I wish you'd stop talking about it!" With that I picked up my beer and chugged it down as fast as I could. "See you," I told him in a nasty voice and started walking out.

I was counting my steps as I walked. All the time every fiber of my body was waiting for him to call out, "Up against the wall, buddy, it's the Secret Service."

Nothing. He bought it. He didn't follow me. I didn't go near the rally. Instead I walked around the block and approached the same corner from a different direction. And there he was, once more standing on the corner, staring straight ahead. Just waiting and watching.

SueEllen was waiting up for me when I came home. She asked me how I liked his speech. "It was an interesting talk," I told her. I was doing enough worrying for two people; I didn't see any reason to bother her with it. After she went to sleep I lay awake all night, too hyper to even close my eyes. I just kept thinking, turning over and over in my mind how close it was. What a thin line separated me from a lifetime behind bars.

The more time passed in Cleveland, the itchier I got. Every time anyone looked at me with more than a casual glance, I began to worry. I began to see problems where none existed. Instead of feeling more secure as time went on, I felt in more danger. I realized I was becoming paranoid, but I also knew that just because I was paranoid didn't mean people weren't after me.

Finally, near the end of October, 1964, I had enough of Cleveland. SueEllen and I were having dinner in the apartment one night and I brought up the subject of moving.

"Look, honey," I said, "why don't we split from this place? I got to leave at the end of the year anyway, so why don't we just go now?"

"Are you worried about something?"

"Nothing in particular, I just don't feel comfortable. I'd really like to take off somewhere."

She considered it and then asked, "Where do you want to go?"

I'd been trying to figure that one out for quite awhile. I rejected one large city after another, and as a fugitive you're limited to large cities with big labor pools if you want to stay free. Then I began to focus on Canada. Once, before I met SueEllen, I had gone across the border to Windsor, Ontario, one weekend. I didn't need a passport or any identification. The border guards simply ask, "Where were you born?" and "When are you coming back?" and that was it. Also, Canada appealed to me as being as far away from Orlando as you could go.

"Toronto," I told her.

She was a Canadian citizen and I thought she'd like the idea of going home. But she surprised me.

"I don't want to go back," she said.

A fugitive doesn't have much choice. "SueEllen, I do love you very much," I told her, "but I've got to get out of the country for awhile. I'm going to Toronto whether you come with me or not, but you know I'd like you along with me."

She thought about it almost a full day, and then she agreed to go with me. I knew she didn't really want to go home, she was happy in Cleveland, but I also knew she didn't want to lose me. We got real high that night, toasting our soon-to-be new free life.

There was one more thing I just had to do before we left, communicate with my family. The fact that I left in the darkness of night without a word to anyone had just been eating me up alive. I wanted my boys to know that I left because I had to, not because I didn't love them. This trip to Canada offered me the perfect, safe way to finally communicate with them.

Our bus left Cleveland and stopped briefly in Buffalo, New York, before going on to Toronto. I knew I couldn't mail the letters from Cleveland and I knew I couldn't mail them from Toronto. I devised this reverse psychology plan to fool the authorities. I explained the whole situation to SueEllen and asked her to write exactly what I dictated. She did.

The first letter went to the chief of the Orlando Police Department. "Dear Chief," she wrote, "I've been living with Jack Clouser up in Canada and he told me one day that he used to be a policeman in your department. He says he hated all of you and he's coming back with a trunkful of dynamite to blow you all up." She signed a fictitious name.

Then I wrote a letter to Mike Trestlee. "Dear Mike," I said nicely, "you crud. You lying crud. Your ass is bought and paid for, and soon you gonna buy it all." None of this was true, of course. I did want to make Trestlee suffer, to be watching shadows, but my real reason was to attract the attention of the authorities. My thinking was, if I mailed these threatening letters from Buffalo, the authorities would assume I'd been hiding out in Canada and was coming back to the United States to wreak havoc in Florida. Because they already believed I was crazy, I knew they would take the letters seriously.

The real purpose of these letters was to enable me to write to my family. I wrote one to my parents and a second one to another close friend of mine from prison. I didn't want to write directly to my boys because I wasn't sure June would give them my letter. "Please find my two sons," I wrote to my friend, "and as best you can explain to a five-year-old and a four-year-old, try to make them understand that their father can't be with them. Tell them that I love them with all my heart, and maybe someday, someday, this will all work out."

The authorities did indeed take my letters seriously. Far too seriously for my own safety, as I was soon to find out.

The immigration officer came on the bus at the Canadian border. He was slowly working his way toward the rear of the bus, where SueEllen and I were sitting. This is a routine procedure, I kept telling myself, routine. But I was fully aware that one small slip-up during any of the thousands of "routine procedures" most people go through every day of their lives would mean the end of my freedom.

"May I see your tickets, please," he asked when he reached us.

I handed over our two one-way tickets to Toronto.

He looked at them, then said, "You're American citizens, aren't you?"

I nodded. "Yes, this is my wife."

"You don't have a return ticket."

"Well, my wife is a Canadian citizen and she has dual citizenship. We're going to visit some of her friends and relatives in Canada and don't know exactly how long we're going to stay."

It was completely logical. And also false.

"You know, you're only allowed six months in Canada," he said. "Then you'll have to register or go back to the U.S."

"No problem," I assured him. "We'll be back long before six months."

Actually I wasn't so sure about that. Canada really appealed to me as a place to start a new life. If I could get myself a job, establish an identity, and get used to the Canadian people, there was a good chance I would never return to the United States.

Toronto in the winter is truly beautiful. It's dry, snowy white, and well lit by pretty street lamps. The people smile and are very friendly. SueEllen and I found a small flat in Bathurst, the Italian section of the city. She went out and found a job almost immediately. I filed for my work card.

Nobody can work in Canada without this card, their equivalent to the American social security card. I made up my story and walked into the registry office. I was Robert Jason Ryan. I had been born in Windsor, Ontario, and my parents took me to the States as a baby. I lived there my entire life and only recently decided to return home. I made up a mother and father and even an address. It was a small gamble that they wouldn't check.

Ten days later my work card arrived in the mail. I celebrated by going directly to the day-labor pool. I sat the entire day, and part of the next. But finally someone yelled out, "Ryan," and I answered in my Irish accent, "Aye! Ryan here!" They sent me to a ceramic tile factory, where I drove the fork lift.

SueEllen and I bought a secondhand television set and we'd cuddle up at night and watch TV and make love. I was starting to believe that I really could make a home for myself in Canada. I was getting comfortable. That's when disaster struck.

I come home from work one evening and I can tell immediately that something is wrong. SueEllen is all fidgety and nervous and keeps turning her back on me and walking away.

"What's going on?" I kept demanding. "C'mon, what's wrong?"

"You're gonna be angry," she said in a meek voice.

"I'm not gonna be angry. Just tell me what the problem is."

She took a deep breath. "Well, I wrote my sister a letter and—"

"Jesus Christ! I told you not to do that. You can't write your family when you go with me. Didn't I tell you that? Didn't I?"

"I just wrote to keep in touch, that's all. I didn't mean to do any harm."

"Tell me what happened."

She started crying. "My sister, she gave our address to my husband. He's on his way up here."

I sat down. Then I looked at her coldly and said, "Do you realize what you've done? When your husband gets here either he's gonna kill me or I'm gonna kill him. Either way I'm in a hassle and I cannot afford that hassle. No way." I tried to figure out what to do. "We got to go, man, we got to split."

She wasn't at all upset by that. When I look back at that now I believe this is what she wanted. She hated Canada.

"Let's go back to Cleveland," she pleaded.

"Cleveland your ass," I told her. "There's no way I can go back to Cleveland." I stayed awake all night trying to figure out where to go. New York, I finally decided. It would be a good place to hide until I made other plans. Back to New York City, this time with a little more money, some solid Canadian identification, and a very pretty redhead.

I went to the station to buy the bus tickets. On the way I made a very silly decision. Violating my number one rule, I called my family home in Knoxville, Tennessee. My mother answered the telephone.

"Mother," I said, "this is your son Jack."

I could hear her catch her breath on the other end of the line. "I have no son. He's dead."

"Mother, would you stop this bullshit?" I told her. "What's wrong with you? I'm talking."

She started crying softly into the phone. "Where are you?"

"Omaha, Nebraska," I lied. "What's going on down there?"

"Don't you know?"

I didn't know anything.

"The FBI placed you back on their top ten list after you mailed those letters about the dynamite."

"Oh, Christ," I said, more to myself than to her. That was something I hadn't expected. I knew how well the wanted posters were circulated. It was going to make my running just that much more difficult.

"And this phone is tapped, Jack, they're listening to everything we say."

That didn't surprise me. But then, on the spur of the moment, without even thinking about what I was saying, I told my mother, "I got news for you and whoever's listening. I'm tired, tired of running. I'm ready to give myself up. I only ask one thing. I am very much in love with a girl, Mother. If you would let her come to Tennessee and live with you, I'll give myself up and try to get this thing straightened out."

I really don't know if I meant what I was saying. The words just seemed to run out of my mouth, and if she had agreed, I'm not sure exactly what I would have done. It turned out I didn't have to worry about it.

"Oh, Jack, I'm tired of your whores," my mother said. "There's no way I want anything to do with any more of them."

There was a long silence. Neither of us said a word.

Then she continued with finality, "You don't live any more for me. You just don't exist."

"Well, thanks a lot, Mother. Good-bye." I sat there in that phone booth, staring at the black box, thoughts racing in and out of my mind. My own mother! Had I been that terrible? Had I hurt people so badly? Had I been that disloyal to my family?

"You gonna use the phone, mister?"

84

I looked up and snapped back into reality. I had no idea how long I'd been sitting there, thinking.

That was the last contact I ever had with my mother.

SueEllen and I hit the road again immediately. I had never done so much traveling in my life. I was brought up to establish roots, to stay in one place as much as possible. This transient living was totally new to me. I realized it was necessary, but I hadn't gotten used to it yet. I'm not sure I ever did.

We only stayed in New York long enough for a quick talk with my friend Frank Boswell. "Listen," I shouted into the telephone, "I'm back in New York with my girl friend. I'm holding your hundred bucks, you know, and I'd like to pay you back."

"Hey, look," he told me, "I'm gonna make that a gift to you. I'm also gonna give you some good advice. Don't stay around town. The cops are making the place hot. They're coming down on everybody. It just ain't a good idea to be around."

Especially with my photograph hanging in every post office in the United States, I thought to myself.

"I guess you're right, Frank," I agreed. "Listen, I did use your social security number like you told me, and I quit at the end of the year. I'll send it back to you. I don't want to use it any more."

"Just throw it away," he said. "I'll get another one." We hung up as friends, and Frank Boswell moved out of my life forever.

Where to go? Where to go? "Cleveland," SueEllen begged.

"I can't go back there," I told her. "I've got no identification." I knew I couldn't use Boswell any more and I was afraid to use my Canadian IDs issued to Robert Jason Ryan. I guessed the police had traced my call to my mother back to Toronto. If they dug deep enough they could have the name Ryan on the wire to every city in the country within hours.

"You could use my husband's name," SueEllen said.

"That's not exactly so bright," I said sarcastically. "What's he gonna use?"

She smiled. "Nothing. He's up in Canada looking for us!"

That wasn't exactly so stupid.

I figured I would only stay in Cleveland a short time, long enough to make some money, but not so long that the IRS pegged me from tax forms. I used SueEllen's husband's social security number and reported for work at a day-labor pool all the way across town from where we used to live. They gave me a job as a fork lift operator in a warehouse. It was clean, sweaty, hard work and I really enjoyed it. In fact, I really liked Cleveland. It's a good place.

On the first Friday night in April 1965, I picked up my check and went home. It started out to be a typical, relaxing Friday evening. SueEllen and I planned to have an early, easy dinner and then go downtown and catch a movie. But just as we were set to walk out the door I decided to hang back a few minutes and catch the early news. I turned on the TV set, and I got the greatest shock of my entire life.

"My God," I said, as I lowered myself slowly into the big living room chair. A picture of me taken soon after I joined the Orlando police force was flashed on the screen and the announcer said, "This is a special news item. The Federal Bureau of Investigation announced today that William Clouser"—he didn't even say John—"is known to be in the Cleveland area. Clouser is wanted in the state of Florida for armed robbery. He escaped from a Florida mental hospital on April the second of last year, where he had been adjudged legally insane. He is an expert pistol shot, is proficient at judo, and must be considered armed and extremely dangerous. He has vowed never to be taken alive. Anyone knowing about his present whereabouts is urged to contact the local FBI office or Cleveland police. Do not attempt to take any action on your own. Repeat, do not attempt to take any action on your own."

I sat in that chair, petrified. Too many people in Cleveland knew me, even with my darkened hair, mustache, and glasses. Somebody would realize that Frank Boswell was really William Clouser. I couldn't believe they had found me. But how? How? The real Frank Boswell in New York? No way he'd cooperate with the police. His wife? She didn't even know I was in Cleveland. SueEllen? The woman I loved? Absolutely no way.

I just couldn't figure it out. And I really wasn't interested in wasting time trying to. I had to get out of Cleveland. Very quickly.

SueEllen was hysterical. She couldn't stop crying and shaking. I knew she'd be no help to me if I couldn't get her to pull herself together, and I knew how badly I needed her help.

"Listen," I said, "c'mon, listen to me. The damage is done. Now I'm trapped and you've got to help me get out of here. Understand?"

"I'm so sorry," she just kept saying over and over.

"I know you are, honey, but you've got to get ahold of yourself. If we're gonna get out of here, I need you to act really cool." I knew I was going to have to show her exactly what I meant. "Believe me, I've been through this before and it's not that bad. You'd be surprised how difficult it is to put together a picture and a person you know. Specially the way I look now."

"I'm so sorry."

"I know, I know. Now put your coat on, because we're going to the movies."

"We can't go outsi—"

"Just put your damn coat on! I don't have time to explain everything to you. Do you trust me?"

She didn't answer.

"Do you trust me?" I said a little louder.

"Yes," she said quietly.

We started walking downtown. I specifically picked the main streets for us to walk on. It was a desperate gamble on my part but I had no choice. Without SueEllen I was finished, and SueEllen was useless the way she was. Every time she saw a policeman, or a car stopped too suddenly, or she heard a loud noise, she would jump and then start shaking again. I had to show her that I wasn't afraid of the danger. I had to prove we could get out of this trouble. I spotted a policeman just standing on a corner and instantly made my decision.

"I'm going to show you something. Go in here," I ordered, pointing to a doorway. "I'm walking across the street to talk to that policeman."

"Oh, no! Please don't do that. I know he'll recognize you."

"He's not going to recognize anybody," I said with as much confidence as I could muster. "He knows as well as anybody that no man on the top ten most wanted list is going to be outside walking on the streets. And if he was, he's definitely not going to be asking a cop for directions. Watch."

I didn't know if I was doing the right thing, but I didn't feel I had much choice. I walked directly across the street, keeping my eyes on the cop the entire way. I could see he was bored stiff from standing on that corner.

"Pardon me, officer. Can you tell me where the Putnam Cafeteria is?"

"It's on Putnam Street," he told me in a bored voice. As he pointed out the directions he never even looked at me square. I thanked him and picked up SueEllen.

"I told you," I said, "there's nothing to worry about. We just have to be smart and cool. Now you've got to stop this shaking and trembling. You've got to believe in me, like I believe in myself."

In a meek voice she said, "I do believe in you."
I didn't believe her at all.

We sat through the movie, we didn't really watch it. Both of us were too wrapped up in our thoughts to pay any attention to what was going on in front of us. One solid year I had managed to stay loose, almost a year to the day. And now they were coming down on me. I always knew it was possible, but I never really thought it would happen. I was too good, too careful, too smart to get caught. Now they had me.

Slowly, I managed to shift my thinking toward developing an escape plan. My best hope was to convince the FBI that they were wrong, that I really was not in Cleveland. Then, if they lowered their guard, I could dash out. I knew it was a long shot, but I had just about run out of sure things.

The way to prove to the FBI that I wasn't in Cleveland was to prove to them that I was somewhere else. And if I couldn't be somewhere else, at least my postmark could. So I sat down and wrote a good long letter to J. Edgar Hoover.

"Dear Mr. Hoover," it began. "Roses are red, violets are blue, you're not smart enough to catch me, so nuts to you!" Then I spent three more pages telling Hoover that I shouldn't be on the top ten, that his men were hounding me, and that he should worry about himself, why he feels it's necessary to sleep with a night light and a teddy bear, rather than chasing me. "I haven't done anything," I finished. "Just leave me alone, let me live my life in peace."

I knew the letter was going to infuriate Hoover. That was exactly what I wanted. I wanted the FBI to feel that a man would have to be crazy to challenge Hoover like that—crazy enough to forget that letters get postmarked from the point they are mailed at.

Once the letter was written, the next part was easy. I called the bus station and found out the price of a round-trip ticket to Detroit. I sealed the envelope and handed it to Sue Ellen.

"I want you to go to the bus station," I told her, "and get on the bus to Detroit. When you get there get off, mail this letter, and come home." I kissed her good-bye and said a little prayer for me.

While she was gone I tried to figure out my next move. New York was out. The South was out. The Midwest bored me silly. That left California, and the more I thought about it, the more I liked the idea. Los Angeles was big enough to get lost in. The climate was somewhat like Florida's. There were so many people moving out there, nobody would get suspicious. And I had never been there before. California, I decided, here we come.

"I've made my decision," I explained to SueEllen when she came back from mailing my Detroit letter to the FBI. "As soon as the heat's off, I'm going to the West Coast, and I'd like you to go with me."

She smiled and threw her arms around me. "Yes, yes, yes, yes, yes," she screamed excitedly.

"Wait a second now," I kept talking, "there's more. If you go with me you're going to have to file a divorce against this guy and we'll end this shit once and for all. You'll become a single woman and then we'll get married." I thought that was exactly what she wanted.

I guess I really didn't understand her like I thought I did. She let her arms hang down and didn't even look at me. "I can't do that, Frank. I'm a Catholic, and I can't get a divorce. If I do I'll go to hell."

"Hell! What are you giving me? Goddammit, I don't want to hear any more of that crap."

She started screaming right back at me, word for word, yell for yell. We fought over religion for the entire night, and that was really the end of our relationship. I had called and told my boss I was leaving Cleveland because of a family illness, and SueEllen was afraid to leave me alone. So for ten days we stayed home and hassled over just about everything.

"I love you," I screamed at her, "but we just can't go on like this, you know."

"Just go," she yelled back. "Take all our money and get out."

"If that's the way you want it," I told her, "I'm going without you!"

"That's the way I want it."

Ten days after she mailed the letter from Detroit I packed my traveling bag, put on my glasses, pulled my hat down deep over my eyes, and walked out.

Once I stepped outside the apartment my life with SueEllen was finished completely. I didn't even think about her. My mind was concentrating on what was going to happen at the bus station. It was very possible that I was going to leave the station in the back seat of a police car.

I stood outside the depot almost an hour, trying to case the place, before going in. Fifteen minutes before my bus was scheduled to leave, I took a deep breath, gave a quick glance around to see if cops were in the area, and crossed the street to the entrance.

There was one cop standing in the waiting room. I looked directly at him. For a split second he looked directly back at me, then averted his eyes. This was a trick I had picked up a long time ago; staring directly at a person was almost a guarantee he would look away. People just don't want to make eye-to-eye contact.

When I reached the ticket window I did exactly the same thing, staring right at the ticket seller. "Chicago, one way," I told him. Then I looked slightly over to his right. And there, taped onto the wall about eighteen inches away from his head, was my fugitive poster, with that old Orlando photo on it. I was fascinated, but I tried not to look too hard or too long. The ticket seller must have picked up something because he stopped what he was doing and looked at me and then turned and looked at the poster.

I didn't move. I hardly breathed.

He did it again. First me, then the poster. It was really obvious he was trying to decide if I was the crazy psychopath from Florida. I knew I had to do something to take his mind off that photograph.

So I did the simplest thing of all. I took off my hat.

That satisfied his curiosity. He went back to making out my ticket and I started breathing regularly again. I had a pretty good idea of what he was thinking: If I was that fugitive I would have never taken my hat off and let him see my whole face. He handed me my ticket, saying, "One to Chicago."

In Chicago I checked into a transit flophouse and shaved off my mustache. Then I caught a Trailways to Denver. In Denver I took the time to go to a barber and all my hair came off, leaving me with a nice, dark crewcut. Finally I took my glasses off and put them in the case. My face looked very different than it had on the wanted poster the FBI was circulating. And, because I hadn't been eating well the past month and had lost weight, my body was also very different than the poster described. My disguise was almost complete.

When I reached Los Angeles I wore my hat as I checked into a cheap hotel. The very first thing I did was buy some peroxide. I went up to the roof of the building and put a certain amount of the peroxide on my hair. The sun dried it into a nice red color. When I walked out of that place to look for work I had a red crewcut, no beard, no mustache, I was skinny, and I wasn't wearing glasses. I looked like an entirely new person.

And that new person was named James Alvin Ripley.

90

John William Clouser was dead. Robert Jason Ryan was dead. Frank Boswell was dead. That left me in Los Angeles with no name, no identification, and almost no money. I arbitrarily picked the name James Alvin Ripley, the James Alvin after someone I knew in prison, the Ripley from "Believe It or Not."

I decided to do exactly the reverse of what I had done in Canada. I went to the social security office and explained that I was a Canadian citizen in Los Angeles visiting, and I was so impressed that I planned to apply to immigrate. In the meantime I needed a social security card to work. Again I made up a phony life history.

Then I waited. My money was almost completely gone and I was down to one meal a day. One week passed. Maybe they were checking me too thoroughly. Eight days. Then the weekend. Finally on Monday it arrived, that beautiful, gorgeous card. James A. Ripley lives!

So, armed with my brand-new social security card and my rent receipt, I hit the Seventh Street labor hall. Same routine as everywhere else in the country: name, social security number, address, sitting around. This time I sat around for just about an hour before I was sent out on a job. They really needed workers out there and I was a good one. I got out every day, sometimes six days a week if they needed Saturday workers. I never refused a job, ever. I wanted to build up my money and I would have worked on Sunday if they had given me the opportunity.

My expenses were pretty small and I wasn't blowing much on anything but the bare essentials, so I was building up a small bankroll. Actually it was more of a pocketroll, because I had to keep all the money I had in my pocket. That is another inconvenience of being on the run. You can't use the banks. There's no way of knowing when you're going to need every cent you can get your hands on right away.

Los Angeles was fine. I liked the climate and the people seemed decent. The prices weren't too high and, best of all, the police seemed to mind their own business. I was there almost two full months before I had my first run-in with the law.

One Saturday afternoon I was sitting in the main park in Los Angeles, Pershing Square. This is a strange place full of weird people. There were women evangelists, people carrying signs around, and even some little guy running through the park screaming, "Beethoven was one too! Beethoven was one too!"

Sitting on a bench, eyes closed, the sun on my face, I was easily one of the straightest people there—nice pants, clean T-shirt, just listening to everything around me. It felt so very good.

All of a sudden I felt somebody shaking my arm. I opened my eyes and there, looking down at me, was a Los Angeles policeman.

"Yes, sir?" I asked as calmly as I could. "What can I do for you?"

He answered just as calmly, "Would you come with me, please?"

For one brief second I looked around, thinking I might make a run for it. If he made me as a fugitive I had no choice, but I wasn't sure of anything. "Certainly," I told him.

He walked behind me and directed me to a staircase in the middle of the park. As we walked along, he picked up three more men, just as he had snapped me up. When that happened, I knew he didn't know who I was. Now all I had to do was talk him out of whatever foolish notion he had in mind. I couldn't let a little problem become a big downfall.

The five of us walked into a police station located right underneath the park. Inside I was still shaky. Outside I was solid.

"O.K.," he said, "please put all your identification on the table."

The first two men had thick wallets full of everything from drivers' licenses to photographs of their families. I had my social security card, my rent receipt, a library card I had obtained two weeks before, and about $35 in cash. The fourth man had absolutely nothing. *That* made me feel better.

The cop started by asking each of us our full names and writing down our answers. Then he ran an immediate check with the police department. James Alvin Ripley was not wanted for anything at all. But while he's making his phone call I'm working on my story. Boy, have I got one for this guy!

"This all you have?" he asked me.

I nodded.

"Where's your driver's license?"

"I don't drive," I told him politely.

He picked up my social security card and rolled it over in his hand. "This is pretty new, isn't it?"

"Brand-new," I agreed. "I lost my wallet and they just reissued me this card."

He nodded. "O.K., where's your draft card?"

With all the problems I had been through with the FBI and police, this was the first dude who ever asked me about my draft registration. "It was in my other wallet, and—"

"Don't you know it's a violation of federal law to fail to have your draft card on your person?" he interrupted me.

I had no choice but to try to bluff him. "Goddammit!" I screamed as loud as I could. "I served this country for four long years. I fought in Korea against those yellow Commie bastards and I almost got killed there that terrible winter." I lowered my voice and leaned in close. "Let me tell you something, my friend. I was there at the Chosin Reservoir with the Marines when the Chinese attacked. I was fighting for my life and we were running out of ammunition. But I stayed at my machine gun and they came at us, wave after wave of them, running up that hill. You think they had rifles? No, man. Some of them had clubs and hoes, screaming, yelling, blasted out of their minds on opium. But I stayed until they gave us the order to clear out. And then I ran. I ran for my life. I ran thirty miles in temperatures so cold the coffee would freeze in the pots. I ran till my feet were bloody. And I survived and served my country for more than two and a half years after that. And now you got the nerve to ask me where my draft card is?"

That story was totally and completely true. I told it to him almost exactly as it had been told to me by "Willie" Sutton, my friend from Orange County Jail, who actually lived through that battle.

The cop seemed kind of embarrassed. "Don't you have a copy of the card somewhere?"

"Certainly. It's I-D, veteran. And it's back at the family home in Kentucky with all my other important papers."

"I'll tell you what, Red," he began. When he called me that I knew he was looking to be friendly with me. "I'd suggest you write to your family and get that. You should have it with you at all times, even though you are a veteran."

I quickly became calm and compliant. "I'll do that, officer," I agreed. "I didn't know it was important. I'm not a criminal. I'm not breaking any laws. I just wanted to get a little sun."

He didn't answer me, instead he turned to the fourth guy. "You got nothing. We're gonna have to take you downtown and check you out to see who you are." The guy started complaining, but the cop didn't give him a chance. He looked at the three of us and told us we were free to leave.

I stopped long enough to ask what the roundup was about. Were they looking for something in particular?

They weren't. It was just a routine check of new faces.

Now I understood why he picked me out—if there was one thing I had, it was a new face!

For quite awhile after that experience, Los Angeles became just like every other city I had spent time in. I worked hard all day, and at night either watched television or went to local hangouts to meet people. When you're running you really need a friend, I don't care how tough you try to be. And when you're lonely, you sometimes pick the wrong people to get friendly with.

I became pretty close to two dudes I met at the labor hall. One was an ex-paratrooper and one was an ex-federal convict. We had been friends about three weeks when I made the mistake of going out on the town drinking with them.

Up to this point we had just stayed in our apartments drinking, and we drank slow and easy. Outside we were all different, we just started chugging it down. After we'd gone through about ten beers apiece, these guys start hassling people. They met a bus driver who lost a small bet to them and didn't pay and they beat him up bad, just slaughtered him, right there in the bar. As soon as I saw trouble starting, I got up and left the place. I couldn't afford it.

I walked into another bar, and five minutes later, in they came. "Hey, man, where you going?"

I held up the palm of my hand. "Look, I don't want any fighting. Let's just drink and have a good time."

They agreed. So we sit in that second bar and, son of a bitch, they start another fight. In my mind I can see the cops coming. I got up and went to a third bar.

Sure enough, they follow me. And they are drunk worse than I am, which is very drunk. My two friends are loud and looking to start trouble and they start picking on this one customer. Before you know it, the guy comes over and takes a swing at me! I got up and knocked him on his ass. Then I sat down and started drinking again.

I got about half a sip down my throat when somebody tackled me from behind. The whole bar breaks out in a real down-home fight. Chairs are being thrown, bodies are flying over the counter, women are screaming. Part of me is loving every minute of it, but I'm also thinking to myself, You idiot! What the fuck are you doing? Finally it dawned on me that I'd better get out of that place and I took off with my two friends in hot pursuit.

We ran about seven blocks, huffing all the way. Finally we stop to rest and I begin to realize what I had just done. How close I came to going back to jail. And the only people close enough to blame are my paratrooper and my prisoner.

"You fucking guys don't know what you're doing," I screamed at them. "Why do you pick these fights?"

The paratrooper started screaming right back at me.

I wasn't smart enough or sober enough to know the time to quit had arrived. "You fucker. You think you're tough. I'll kick your ass right here, right now." He challenged me right back. So, without thinking too hard, I grabbed him by the shirt on his right shoulder and by his left arm and flipped him over my shoulder onto his ass on the sidewalk.

Thud! He just hit the ground and laid there. He didn't even quiver.

Oh, shit, I thought, now I've really gone and done something. I start bending over him, to see if he's getting up, and his buddy just hauled off and kicked me in the face. I heard my nose smash even before I felt the flow of blood come rushing out. As I hit the ground I somehow realized I had to get up. I tried. The ex-con kicked me down again. Then he kicked me again, and again. Finally, as if he wasn't doing a good enough job himself, his buddy, the ex-paratrooper, managed to get up and start stomping me.

I was finished. I got one hand on my eyes and the other hand on my balls and I just laid there, taking their best shots to every part of my body. They just stomped and kicked me until I could barely hear them. They were about a million miles away and one of them said, "I think we killed him."

"Yeah, he looks dead," the other one said. I couldn't tell which one was which. "Let's go." I heard them start running away.

I just laid there, taking one breath after another, and always a little surprised when the next one filled my lungs. God almighty, I was hurtin'. I have no idea how long I laid there in that gutter. Finally, ever so slowly, I pulled myself to a telephone pole and managed to sit up. I was covered with blood. My once white T-shirt was just ripped right off and my white Levi's were completely red. I kept telling myself, Get up, get up, gotta get home, gotta get home.

Ever so slowly I pulled myself to my feet. I stayed on my feet maybe thirty yards and then collapsed again. I had to get up, I knew I just had to. Somehow I got to my feet and started walking. Boom, back on the ground. The blood was still pouring out of my nose, and my ears had started bleeding too. Finally two cops showed up. I didn't know whether to try to kiss them or run from them. Actually, I couldn't do either.

"What happened?"

I knew what happened, but I wasn't about to tell them. I wouldn't squeal on anyone, no matter what they did to me.

"Two—two strangers jump me. Think they was trying to rob me. They just—just whipped me to death." Getting that out was an effort.

"Can you identify them?"

"No." I *could* have taken them right to their house. "Never seen 'em before."

"O.K.," one of them said to his partner, "let's send this guy to the hospital. Get on the box."

"No. No," I managed to tell them. "No hospital. Want to go home." I knew I was fucked up badly, but I knew I'd feel worse if they took me to the hospital and started asking questions.

"Hey, man, you're gonna bleed to death. We gotta put you in an ambulance."

"I don't want—ambulance. I'm going home."

One of the cops laughed. "Listen, if this dummy wants to die, what do we care? Call him a cab." They did exactly that.

The cab took me back to my apartment, only two blocks away, and I got out and paid him. I couldn't believe how covered with caked blood I was when I looked in the mirror. Still moving slowly, I got in the shower and washed all the blood off. Then I dragged myself into bed. It was just after 2 A.M.

I laid there for four hours. I couldn't get to sleep. Finally, at six, the alarm clock went off and I got up and started putting some clean clothes on. My mind was working like one of the cartoons where the angel is telling the brain one thing and the devil is saying exactly the opposite. I heard voices: "Where the hell are you going?" I asked.

"I'm going to work," I answered.

"So what are you trying to prove?"

"I don't know, but I'm going to prove it."

And I went to work.

96

The dispatcher took one look at my busted-up face and said, "My God, Jim, what the hell happened to you?"

I told him I didn't want to talk about it.

"Well, you can't work like—"

"Just send me out. Don't argue."

Finally he agreed to send me out. I started loading a boxcar at 8 A.M. and I worked until two in the afternoon. Then, simply, I keeled over on my face and passed out. The next thing I remember was being slapped gently awake in the boss's office. He signed my pay ticket for a full day and sent me home. I managed to get back to my place and crawl into bed before I passed out again.

That was on a Friday. I laid in bed without moving all weekend. I didn't eat, didn't drink, didn't move. Every part of my body ached. My nose was broken. Two ribs were smashed. It even hurt to blink my eyes. Finally Monday morning came and I managed to tape myself up tightly and went back to work.

I took a terrible beating, but I learned a very valuable lesson. Never again did I find it important to prove myself to anybody else, because whatever it was I was trying to show the world, I proved it to myself that night. I learned that the way to prove your toughness is not what you can do to somebody else, but what you can take. I took the limit that night.

My "friends" didn't show up at the labor pool for almost a month. Then one day I looked up and there they were. They didn't say a word. I didn't say anything to them. A full day passed. Then a second day. Finally, at the end of the second day, the paratrooper comes up to me and says, "Hey, we were drunk, man. Don't hold it against us. We're not mad at you, we got nothing against you at all."

"Yeah," the other one chimed in, "we like you." I was lucky they didn't love me! "It was just one of those things, you know."

Personally it seemed a little more serious than that. "Well," I said mildly, "if somebody broke your nose and gave you a concussion, wouldn't you be pissed?"

"Yeah," they agreed.

"O.K. Then I'm pissed."

"Man, we just can't go on like this, looking over our shoulders. What are you gonna do about it?"

"When I decide what I'm gonna do," I promised, "you'll be the first to know." And I just walked away from them.

I was growing up on the run, learning about people and learning about myself. I had to admit that the fight was as much, maybe even more, my fault than theirs. I had no business hanging around when they started acting like animals, and I'm the one who started the hassle in the street. The fact that I could admit that was a major breakthrough for me. I was beginning to understand my own shortcomings.

I never settled with them. Occasionally one of them would look at me and I'd smile a knowing smile, like I had something up my sleeve, but I knew I would never try to get even.

Just like in the other cities, because I was such a good worker I eventually was offered a permanent job, this time in a Goodyear Rubber plant. The job was to start in three weeks. I was working hard all day and playing hard all night. Because I would be making a little extra money, I decided to move into a little bigger apartment than my first place. But, just to be on the safe side, I didn't tell a single person I was moving.

Two days after my move I met this gorgeous girl in a bar. She had the most beautiful face, but her body was crippled. We had a few drinks together and I invited her back to my new apartment. She picked up her crutches and we managed to get there.

I fixed some dinner, then we had a few more drinks, and I finally invited her into my bed. She accepted my invitation. When she took off all her clothes I saw she had a truly wonderful body, except that she was bent. She just couldn't straighten up completely. I realized that might slow me down, but I didn't think it could stop me.

We started by engaging in a little foreplay. She had firm, round breasts and I played with them awhile, really turning both of us on. Finally I started to have intercourse with her, but we just couldn't fit together. No matter how hard I tried, we just couldn't make contact. I rolled over her, she rolled over me, we reversed positions, we tried me off the bed and her on, her off and me on, every variation the Chinese wrote about, everything. Nothing.

"What's happening?" I asked, exasperated.

She then told me one of the saddest stories I have ever heard. "I was once an acrobat," she explained, "and a few years ago I had a terrible accident. And whatever happened, the accident affected my— Anyway, I can't have sex any more."

98

"I can't believe it!" I almost cried.

"I wish it wasn't true," she said.

Neither of us could stand the idea of being left high and dry at that point, so we tried a few things, and finally she suggested something that worked O.K. Thank heavens!

In the morning I helped her into a cab and waved good-bye. Having been now almost arrested, badly beaten, and pretty well frustrated, I was not finding California as sunny as I thought it would be.

The worst was still to come—exactly one week later.

10

The Federal Bureau of Investigation claims to be the finest law-enforcement agency in the world. It has thousands of agents, millions of records, huge sums of money, a worldwide communications network, the best scientific laboratories of criminology in the world, the most modern computer technology, and the free aid of millions of Americans in every city and state in the country. And every piece of equipment seemed to be mobilized just to capture me.

I wanted one peaceful night's sleep. I was constantly looking behind me. I never stopped making plans, inventing stories, being careful. Eventually, I knew, they would put their hands on me. The odds were just too much against me, an ex-southern redneck cop who dropped out of college.

The wanted posters were the thing that bothered me most. I had to keep constantly changing my appearance, but there are basic things about the face that can't be changed. One sharp-eyed citizen, maybe a postman or a co-worker or a bar pickup, and I was finished. At least once every three months, no matter where I was, I would make a point of walking into the post office to see if I was still one of the most wanted men in America. The poster was always there. I never spent too much time looking at it because I didn't want to attract attention, but I saw it with very mixed emotions.

The first was anger. I didn't belong on that list with murderers and bombers and kidnappers. According to the poster, Jack Clouser was wanted for transportation of a stolen vehicle across interstate lines, a crime almost not worth mentioning, much less putting me on the list for.

But my second emotion was a sort of perverted pride. I was one of the most sought-after men in America, a desperado. People all over the country knew my name. Me and legends like John Dillinger and Jesse James and Billy the Kid, we all shared the same sort of lonely success.

In our own way, we were all romantic heroes.

One of the top-rated television shows at that time was David Janssen playing Richard Kimble, "The Fugitive." No matter where I was, every Tuesday night I'd find a television set and watch that show. That was me! I wasn't a doctor, like Kimble, but I was a police officer, a professional man, and I could really relate to that show. I found myself comparing notes with Kimble. The producers romanticized the life of a fugitive; Kimble was here, then he's there, and they never explained how difficult it was to travel. And Kimble never had problems with small things like dandruff and granulated eyelids and bleeding gums and halitosis. Kimble never had athlete's foot or ringworm or piles, all things you've got to treat yourself while you're on the run because you can't risk going to a doctor.

The night the series came to an end I was sitting in a bar. Kimble proved his innocence and walked away a free man. I wondered, Where's it going to end for me? I prayed my story would have a happy ending too.

Then this feeling came over me of wanting to tell somebody, anybody, my secret. Maybe the toughest thing I had to do the whole time I was on the run was keep my secret inside. That night more than ever I wanted to shout it out, tell all the other guys in that bar: That's me, I'm The Fugitive. The best law-enforcement agency in the world is after me and I've outsmarted them! They can't catch me!

And then they caught me.

I was working on an assembly line at Goodyear and late in the afternoon I felt a tap on my shoulder. I turned around and a man introduced himself as a Goodyear security officer.

"I'd like you to come with me," he said.

He led me into his office and two plain-looking young men, dressed neatly in jackets and ties, were sitting there waiting for me. I made them as FBI agents immediately. A warning signal flashed on in my mind: Don't touch anything! I knew once they had my fingerprints I was finished.

"I'm Special Agent John Kennerly of the Federal Bureau of Investigation," the first one began, "and this is Special Agent Dick Woods. We'd like to ask you a few questions."

I stared right at him. "O.K.," I told him.

They started with all the simple questions—name, address, social security number, mother's maiden name, former wife's maiden name, date of birth, home town, and on and on. In my own mind I had covered this same territory so many times I had absolutely no trouble answering their questions quickly and what I hoped seemed truthfully. After asking me once they started asking me twice, only this time they changed the order, hoping that I would slip up. I just eased right through.

"If you don't mind my asking," I finally interrupted, "what is all this about? You know, I've got a job to do."

The security man answered, "Don't worry, Mr. Ripley, you'll be paid for your time."

More questions. I carefully kept my hands folded in my lap. They offered me a glass of water and I politely refused. They weren't getting my prints.

Finally Special Agent Woods reached into his jacket pocket and pulled out a copy of my wanted poster. He laid it right down on the desk in front of me and smoothed it out. "Mr. Ripley," he stated flatly, "we have reason to believe that you are this man, John William Clouser."

I just stared at the poster for a few seconds. This whole meeting was like a bad dream coming true. I had no choice. I laughed, right out loud.

"Me? This guy? Are you kidding? You guys think I really look as bad as this dude?" I didn't even give them a chance to answer. I was getting into my well-planned act. I looked at the security officer. "Are these guys kidding me? What is this?"

"Please cooperate with them, Mr. Ripley," he said.

"Look," said Special Agent Kennerly, friendly-like, "if you're not Clouser all you have to do is give us your fingerprints and that'll prove it."

"You guys are really something," I told them. "Now, honestly, do I look anything at all like this man?" How the hell did they find me? I was wondering.

"No," Woods agreed, "you don't look like him. You're redheaded and you've got a crewcut. Now, there's a little resemblance in the mouth and the ears, but your eyes and your facial structure don't look too much like Clouser's."

"See," I told them, "I'm not the guy."

But he went on. "We can settle it all very quickly with your fingerprints. Just let us take—"

I stopped him in mid-sentence. "I'm not giving you my fingerprints." It was a flat, declarative statement.

"Well, why not?" Kennerly asked. "You got something to hide?"

I turned and stared at him. "I got absolutely nothing to hide." I started getting really angry. "You guys make me sick. Ever since I came here you've been persecuting me because of my political beliefs. I just want to be left alone, you know."

"Mr. Ripley, we don't know anything about your political beliefs."

"You know damn well I'm in antiwar and left-wing organizations and you've been hounding me for months!" That would throw them off the track, I hoped. "Don't give me any more shit. You want to charge me? Am I under arrest?"

"Oh, no, Mr. Ripley," Woods said almost apologetically, "you're not under arrest."

"Well, if you want my fingerprints you're gonna have to arrest me to get them. Go ahead, arrest me if you think I'm this guy. Charge me."

"Mr. Ripley," Kennerly said in an almost bored voice, "if you won't cooperate we will just have to assume you have something to hide."

I laughed out loud again. "You can assume any damn thing you want to. But I'm not giving you my prints because I don't like you." I started screaming now. *"I don't like you! Leave me alone!"*

Kennerly was telling me to relax, relax. When they finally did get me sitting back down in the seat, Kennerly tried another approach. "Mr. Ripley, do you have any tattoos?"

I was ready for them. I did have tattoos, a lot more of them than they thought I did. When I was in Raiford I had another prisoner tattoo a panther on my right arm and a heart with a dagger going through it put on my left arm. They had no meaning. Everybody was doing it, so I did.

My wanted poster described both the tattoos on my arms, although the one on my right arm was wrongly listed as having an arrow rather than a dagger going through the heart. I knew these tattoos would be positive identification, so I had had them changed. On my trip to Chicago from Cleveland I had an artist put an alligator over the panther and add some words and flowers to the heart. At some point in Jamaica I had a red rose done on my right chest, I don't even remember, I was so drugged up. And my first week in Los Angeles, I had a local artist do a dragon's head on my left chest.

"Sure," I told them, "I got tattoos." I opened my shirt and showed them the rose and the dragon on my chest.

Kennerly looked at the tattoos and looked at the wanted poster. A look of complete confusion came over his face and, for the first time, I began to have a faint hope that I might actually pull this big bluff off. He examined the tattoos again and checked them with the poster.

"Are these all the tattoos you have?" he asked.

"Yes. These are all I got."

Kennerly turned out to be smarter than he had been acting. "Would you mind taking your shirt off and showing us?"

I went right back into my indignant act. "Goddam it! You ask me if I have any tattoos and I show you my tattoos. I could've said no, but I wanted to cooperate. Well, I showed you the only tattoos I got. I'm sick of this crap. If you have a charge, put it against me." I was really screaming now. "Arrest me! Take me to jail! Take my toe prints! Examine my body for tattoos! Look up my ass and check my piles! Do anything you want. But, lemme tell you something, this is it. I've had it. I'm sick of this shit! I'm not helping you any more." And I sat there, just staring at them.

Kennerly and Woods both apologized and said they were only doing their jobs. They explained why I should cooperate with them. I explained why I wasn't going to. After twenty minutes of ridiculous arguing they told me to return to work. I thanked them and got up.

I knew exactly what they were going to do the minute I left the room. Woods had his fingerprint kit with him and they were going to start dusting for prints. They weren't going to find any. I had been very careful the entire time I was in the room not to touch anything. And when I left I grabbed the doorknob with the cleft between my thumb and forefinger, making sure not to touch it with my fingertips.

It was almost 4 P.M. when I got back to the assembly line. One hour till quitting time. I started working again but there was no way I could concentrate. The FBI had found me. How? Who knew? Who would have told? And now what was going to happen?

About thirty yards in front of me there was an open door, leading to railroad tracks and a maze of other warehouses. I knew I could make it out the door. But I also knew that if I did, it would be an admission of guilt and they'd have the whole area surrounded so quickly I'd never get away. My only real chance was to continue the bluff to the very end.

I looked behind me. The Goodyear security man was trying to hide behind a stack of tires, keeping a careful eye on me. I knew my FBI friends were dusting like crazy in his office. Fifteen minutes passed. Twenty. Twenty-five. Finally all three of them pulled me off the assembly line and back into the office.

We went over all the details again. Fingerprints? No. Tattoos? No. Name? James Alvin Ripley. Address? Social security number? They were very upset. Both of them were young and, I think, relatively inexperienced. My training as a police officer helped me anticipate them every step of the interrogation. After I got indignant one more time, and started screaming about my constitutional rights as a citizen of the United States of America, they told me to go back to work. When I reached the assembly line there were five minutes left in the day. They were the longest five minutes of my life.

Finally, my shift ended. As a group the men from the labor pool climbed onto the bus that took us back to the agency's office. I grabbed a seat right next to the side exit, and pulled my best friend on the assembly line, a young Mexican named Rafael, right down into the seat next to me.

After the bus had gone a few blocks I looked out the back window. Just as I figured, Woods and Kennerly were following us in their private car. They obviously knew the bus was going back to the labor pool so we could be paid, and I guessed the office would be swarming with agents by the time we got there. I had to get off that bus!

"Look, Rafael," I said softly to my Mexican friend, "I can't go into it now, but I'm a federal fugitive. Those two men in the car behind us, they're FBI agents here to arrest me. I gotta get away from them. Can you help me?"

He didn't even hesitate. "Sure, I help," he said, smiling. "What you want?"

It was a simple plan, with little chance of succeeding. "They're two blocks behind us. When we turn the next corner I'm gonna jump out the back door and head for the bar on the corner. Come with me."

"Good," he agreed. It wasn't, but it was the best I had.

We started getting up as the bus reached the corner. As soon as we finished the turn, and were temporarily out of sight of the agents, I pushed the door open and ran the ten yards to the bar at full speed. Rafael was with me every step. We hid inside the door until Woods and Kennerly drove by, and then took off down a back alley. We headed back toward Seventh Street, winding our way through alleys and back lots. Finally we reached the end of the block the labor pool office was on.

"Now," I told Rafael. "Go to the dispatcher and get your day's pay and try to get mine. I'll be sitting right here waiting for you."

"What you do, man?" he wanted to know.

"I'll tell you later," I promised, "but now go and get your money, and find out what's going on at the office." Then I sat in that alley and I waited. I just could not figure out how they found me. It made absolutely no sense at all, but there they were. I did manage to fool them at Goodyear, but jumping off the bus was as good a confession as they could have wanted. If they caught me again I was finished.

I knew I had one very important advantage: the agents did not know where I lived. I had given my new address to absolutely no one, and no one had ever been up there except the crippled pickup. I was positive they figured I'd be going back to my old place.

Rafael returned in about twenty minutes. "Wow," he said. "Lots of men, lots of guns. Dispatcher no can give me your pay, but he tell me to tell you, 'Jim, whatever you done, stay away, because there are so many FBI men around here no can believe it.' I see them myself. Shotgun in the back room, men with shotguns in the bar across the street. The place is full of them. What you want to do?"

"Let's go to the toilet," I told him. I needed a safe place to talk. When we got inside I said, "I'm gonna level with you, Rafael. I'm on the top ten most wanted list for some things I swear I didn't do. I've been writing some letters to Hoover and I think they'd shoot my ass off if they got the chance. Can you help me?"

"Anything, *amigo.*" Three years earlier I thought all Mexicans were stupid, smelly wetbacks. Now I was asking a Mexican to save my life.

The agents would be looking for someone wearing the bright orange shirt I had on when they questioned me at the plant. Rafael had a dull blue one on. We exchanged shirts.

Next I had to cover up my red hair. I gave Rafael two dollars and sent him across the street for something to wear on my head. He came back with a brown leather cap.

"I don't know if I'm gonna make it," I told him, "but if I do, I got you to thank for it. I won't forget you."

We shook hands and I took off.

It took me more than an hour to make what was normally a ten-minute walk to my new apartment. I stayed off the streets as much as I possibly could, sticking to alleys and lots. I didn't know the back way at all, so I sort of felt my way along and got lost a couple of times. But I made it. I slammed the door behind me and double-bolted it. Part one of my escape had been successful. Now all I had to do was get out of the neighborhood and then out of the state, and then out of the country. That's all.

I poured myself a good stiff drink and then I sat down and started shaking. I couldn't believe I had gotten away from them. It was an impossible escape and, so far, it was working. But I was feeling deeper things. I needed help, I wanted somebody to believe in me, to put their arms around me and tell me this was all just a terrible dream.

How could they have found me? I had a new name, good identification, I even looked different. As I sat in that chair, drinking and shaking, I realized, probably for the first time, that there really was no escape. I was going to be a hunted man, living in fear, until they caught me or I died.

I poured myself another drink. I wasn't about to give up. I had survived too many blows to quit. I had to get out of town.

I turned on both the radio and the television set, constantly switching channels, trying to pick up the news. Had the FBI put me on the air? I played with the dials for about twenty minutes. Nothing. Then I turned the TV off and turned the volume down on the radio.

For the first time I heard the sirens.

It's a fire, I thought at first. But they were too loud and too constant. So I took the elevator to the roof of my building and looked out.

It wasn't fire trucks at all.

The whole neighborhood was ringed with black-and-white police cars, motorcycles, and police buses. I stood up on that roof just watching the cars moving in out of the surrounding blocks. They didn't know where I was, but they somehow knew I was in the neighborhood.

Now they really had me good. I couldn't get out of the neighborhood. The whole area was cordoned off. They were closing in on me.

I went downstairs to my apartment and sat in my one comfortable chair and poured myself another drink. Well, I said to myself, if they're going to take me, they're going to take me with a big heat on.

By six-thirty the house-to-house search had started, and I knew they were slowly but positively working their way toward my block, my building, my front door. I wasn't armed, I wasn't going to resist. When they said, "Stick 'em up," all I was going to ask was, "How high?"

The radio played softly in the background and I put away two-thirds of a bottle of vodka. While I was drinking, I started thinking over the last two years. I had come so far from Orlando and my upbringing, I was finally beginning to understand what my life was all about, and now it was going to be cut off. It just didn't seem fair.

I held my drink high to the sky and started talking out loud. "Well, God, I guess this is it. There'll be no ten years of freedom after all. You're sending me back to those rednecks. God, I need a miracle to get out of this one." And then I rambled on a bit more.

After I was silent for a short while I turned the radio louder. The sirens were still blaring through the streets and I was trying to drown them out. At first the station played pleasant listening music and I didn't pay too much attention. Then they interrupted the program for a special news bulletin.

Here it comes, I thought to myself. Attention, Los Angeles, a maniac named John William Clouser is walking the streets.

I was completely wrong.

Street fighting and huge fires had broken out in Watts, Los Angeles' black ghetto, said the radio, and policemen all over the city were being ordered to return to duty. Almost all police cars on duty were being sent into the area.

The Watts riots had started.

"God," I said out loud because I was so stunned, "this is my chance. It's happened. My miracle."

God had come through again.

I went up to the roof again. The black-and-white police cars were pulling out. Policemen were running down the streets and hopping into the back of patrol cars. It looked like the beginning of a war.

The radio continued to broadcast news. The riots were growing. More police were streaming into the area. Firemen were trying to get into the area to fight the fires. I knew I had to move fast. The FBI hadn't had time to pick up where the cops had left off. While the city was still in a state of shock and confusion, I had to get out of there. I packed as many belongings as I could in one bag, leaving behind everything else I had picked up—dishes, silverware, good clothes. For the fourth time I was cleaned out.

I went up to the roof and checked one more time. There wasn't a cop in sight. Off in the distance I could see a tiny black cloud rising into the sky—that was Watts burning. I was too excited for myself to even think about feeling sorry for the people. It looked like I was about to pull off one of the great nonviolent escapes of all time. I just had to maintain cool.

I pulled my hat down over my eyes, picked up my bag, hailed a cab, and headed for the Greyhound station. I didn't even hesitate before going in. If they were waiting for me there, so be it, but I just couldn't believe I had come so far to have it end there.

There was one uniformed policeman inside, and he was trying to wake up a drunk. I walked right by him and bought a ticket for San Diego.

Twenty minutes later I was on my way out of town.

11　　I had to get away from the constant pressure, I had to get some relief from the constant worrying, I needed a place I could relax. And that meant leaving the country.

Rafael had told me about a town in Mexico. "Dreamland," he called it. It's a small village four hours by boat from Puerto Vallarta, and it exists mainly for people trying to get away from something. More than half the residents, he told me, were Americans who didn't want to be found. For $40 a month you could get a hacienda, two meals a day, and a maid to both clean the hacienda and sleep with you. I had saved about $150. "Dreamland" sounded like the perfect place, if it actually existed.

I stopped in San Diego for three days, just in case the FBI was smart enough to watch the Mexican border. The newspapers were full of stories about the riots, but there wasn't a single word about the Florida Fox. I wasn't at all surprised. If the FBI had captured me it would have been front-page news, but they weren't about to advertise their failures. I was just as glad; I didn't feel I needed the publicity.

I laid in my hotel room the whole three days, and once the shock of almost being captured wore off, a deep depression set in. I had taken every precaution I could think of, and still they managed to track me down. Unbelievable. I had been on the run for two years and I was absolutely no better off than I had been the first day. My mistake, I began to realize, was not planning far enough ahead. I was always looking at the next day and the next week, when I should have been thinking about a lifetime as a fugitive.

What I had to do, I finally understood, was firmly establish myself as another person. That meant the whole works—birth certificate, driver's license, receipts, and most important of all, a brand-new social security number issued to me and used by nobody else. Getting this identification would be difficult, maybe impossible. But I realized that if I was ever going to be able to live any sort of normal life again, this was the only way.

I walked across the border on Sunday, during the mad rush of Americans to the bullfights in Tijuana, with absolutely no problems. I took a cab to Tijuana and checked into a hotel. The next morning I met two Mexicans driving south and hitched a ride with them to Puerto Vallarta. From there I asked some questions and paid some money and that same day I was on a boat to Dreamland.

Dreamland is set right on the ocean and it is the closest thing to paradise I've ever seen. It is surrounded by dense jungle and totally inaccessible by land. The whole town consists of cantinas, one general store, dozens of little cottages, and a large number of attractive Mexican girls.

As my Mexican friend told me, the place was crammed full of Americans. Half of them were trying to escape from themselves, the other half claimed to be escaping the law. We had all types in town—bond jumpers, bank robbers, alimony-payment dropouts, sex deviates, political activists, and me, the certified psychopath. My plan was to stay in town until my hair grew in and the blond color returned, and I had time to grow a mustache and maybe even add a little weight.

I have always been a good small-stakes poker player, and during my stay in Mexico I became a great one. Myself and some other Americans played almost every day, all day, with a bottle on the table and our girls at our sides. The girl at my side was Clara, who came with my $40 hacienda.

Clara wasn't particularly attractive, but we developed a wonderful relationship. She was only happy when she was with me and doing things to make me happy. One afternoon she took me by the hand into the jungle and part way up the side of the mountain. We came out into a clearing and there was the most beautiful gorgeous waterfall on the face of the earth. I just stood there and stared at the tons of water charging down over the cliff and into the small lake below. It was hard to believe that John William Clouser, not-so-smart hick from the deep South, was standing in paradise. The FBI was long years behind me.

After three months of play I was ready to start traveling again. I was running out of money and I didn't want to be stranded in Mexico without cash. I had never really adjusted to the water and constantly had diarrhea. And I was getting bored with beach, cards, women, and wine every single day. Dreamland had been wonderful, but even paradise can get dull after awhile.

The sun had bleached my once-red hair back to its original blond. The crewcut was just a barber's memory. My mustache was back, this time with a goatee. And, more important, I had gotten time to relax and make some real plans.

I knew my first job was to get some real identification, something that applied to me and no one else. But I also understood that I was in the middle of one of the great adventures left in America. I was

111

playing the most dangerous game in the world, with my life as the stakes. I didn't choose to play, and I would have quit if I had the chance, but as long as I stayed free I resolved to see my plight as a great adventure. In modern society the individual really doesn't have too much of a chance to do anything without machines watching him, helping him, or recording him. Now I was playing against the machines; the machines of the FBI, the Internal Revenue, the social security, all the machines that reduce people to numbers and take away their names. I was caught in the middle: no number, but also no name.

I was relaxed, ready to step back into my adventure. Instead of running from places, I was going to pick my destinations and run to them. As long as I was moving, I might as well see the most beautiful sights and do those things I really wanted. I had been on the defensive too long, now I was ready to take the offense.

I retraced my steps to Tijuana and again walked over the border on Sunday. The customs people asked if I was an American citizen. When I told them that I was, they let me pass without even asking for any identification. My destination was Hawaii, by way of San Francisco. The reason was simple: I wanted to go there. Now all I needed was the cash for a plane ticket.

First I had to get to San Francisco. I took the bus again, and went whizzing right past Los Angeles, not even stopping long enough to spit on the sidewalk. I had no ambition to ever go back there.

When we reached San Francisco I followed my usual pattern by checking into a local fleabag and hitting the local bars. The second day I was there I met this good old southern boy in one of the joints and we spent a large number of hours toasting the Confederacy and General Lee. We got to talking about ourselves and my tongue got very loose and I told him the truth: this truth was that I was broke and trying to raise some money to get to Cincinnati, where my ailing sister lived. He believed my story and invited me to move into his apartment until I raised the needed cash.

After I had been with him for ten days he knew my problem wasn't an ailing sister in Cincinnati. I didn't have any identification, so I couldn't look for a job. He got a little unhappy about me hanging around the house all day, so I had no choice but to tell him the real truth.

"I'm going to give it to you straight this time," I told him. "I've got no sister in Cincinnati. See, I deserted my wife and children and I've

112

got thousands of dollars of alimony hanging over my head. I just want to go off somewhere and start a new life. And that's the truth!"

He was very upset. "Why did you have to lie to me?" he almost pleaded. "I'm a divorced man myself and I know how unfair the laws are. I'm gonna help you all I can!" His name was Sam Wilson, and help me he did. He gave me a photostat of his birth certificate, an *Encyclopaedia Britannica* salesman's identification card, and a membership card in the Highlife Nightclub. "Just use these until you get straightened out," he offered.

While he was handing me the ID I saw his social security card and did my best to memorize the number. I went right into the bathroom and wrote it down. If I needed Sam Wilson's number later, I would have it, and Sam wouldn't get hurt. The worst thing that could happen was he'd have some extra money in his social security account.

Once I had some cards, I felt safer being on the streets. But this time, instead of hitting the day-labor pool, I decided to try my luck. I had won some money gambling in Dreamland and gone so far as to develop a "system" of my own. I took Trailways' Gamblers' Special to Reno, a one-day trip for $7, and tested my theory on the roulette wheel.

With the money I still had saved, plus what I borrowed from Sam Wilson, I got there with $37 in my pocket. If my thing worked the first time, I'd have some money; if it didn't, I was in trouble once again. I bought one five-dollar chip, one ten-dollar chip, and one twenty-dollar chip.

My "system" deals with red and black only on the wheel, forget the numbers. You just stand there and watch the wheel and wait. As soon as the same color comes up four times in a row, you place your bet on the other color. For example, if it comes up red four consecutive spins, you bet black for the fifth. If it still comes up red, then you have to double your bet, in my case ten dollars. And if it still doesn't come up, which means six in a row of the same color, you have to double once again.

If it doesn't come up one time in seven, you better forget it, because the law of averages should guarantee black will come up one time in seven. That was my theory.

It worked! I played it in four different gambling casinos and it worked in every one. I didn't make a lot of money because I didn't have too much money to play with, and waiting until the same color comes up four consecutive times can mean a long wait between bets, but by midnight I was more than one hundred dollars ahead, the cost of a Western Airlines ticket to Honolulu. There was still two hours until the Trailways Special left for San Francisco, but I stopped betting. I won what I came for.

I was really feeling exhilarated from the gambling and winning. As soon as I got back to San Francisco I was going to give Sam Wilson his money back, thank him for helping me, and take off on a new adventure. I sat in a bar waiting for the bus to leave, and I started thinking: You fucking J. Edgar Hoover, this is it. I'm leaving the mainland for awhile now.

The more I think, the angrier I get, and finally I decide to write him again. "Boy, did I make fools of your guys in Los Angeles," I wrote. "You had me, man, and I got away from you. What a bunch of buffoons. What a bunch of phony bunglers." The letter went from intelligent to almost incoherent. And, toward the end, it got sentimental. "I'm getting a little tired," I wrote on the third page. "If there's any chance I could surrender and have all these charges dropped, I'd do it. If there's any chance of this at all put an ad in the personal column of the *Cleveland Press*, the *New York Times*, the *Los Angeles Times,* and the *Chicago Sun*, saying, 'Jack. We've received your offer and it's accepted.' I'll make contact."

The *Los Angeles Times* was sold in Honolulu and I knew I could check it there. If the ad had been in the paper I'm not sure exactly what I would have done. It was a decision I was never forced to make, because the ad didn't appear.

After writing to my friend Hoover I decided to write to my family. I wrote one letter to my sons and a second letter to my mother and sister, telling everyone I was still alive, free, and relatively healthy. I sent my sister a few poems I had scribbled down during my travels. I wished I could have been with her when the letters arrived, I know it must have really surprised her that muscle-bound, football-crazy Jack spent time writing poems. It certainly surprised me when I started.

I put all three letters in one large envelope and sent them to a lawyer friend in Orlando, requesting him to put them in the mail from down there. If he did what I asked and put them through, the Orlando postmark must have blown old J. Edgar Hoover's mind. The FBI was looking all over America for me and I'm home free in Orlando! Even if my lawyer handed the letter directly to the FBI, I was still safe. My letter to him had a Reno, Nevada, postmark, and I'd be long out of there by the time it reached him.

In fact, I must have already been in beautiful Hawaii by the time he received it.

I fell in love with Honolulu the first minute I saw it. It was as exotic and unusual as all that I ever read about it promised. I rented a small room in a sort of dormitory for $20 a week, right in the center of Waikiki, a place called the Jungle. The Jungle is to Hawaii what Greenwich Village is to New York, Haight-Ashbury was to San Francisco, and Taos is to New Mexico. All the poets, painters, writers, philosophers, and simple dropouts congregate in the area, making it always exciting and interesting.

The Jungle is also the homosexual and transvestite center of the island. One thing that immediately struck me different about Honolulu than any place I had ever been before was that everything was open and accepted. The transvestites walked the streets in broad daylight and no one gave them a hard time. In fact, the only law regarding these men who dressed up in women's clothes was that they had to wear little signs outside their dresses identifying them as males. It was quite a shock to me seeing attractive-looking chicks wearing signs that said, "Male," or "I am a boy."

I spent the first week just getting accustomed to Waikiki. The girls were mostly of mixed blood and very pretty. The city was beautiful. And, at that time, prices were somewhat reasonable.

Once my money started slowing down I went to the fugitive's friend, the labor pool, and registered as Sam Wilson. Right away they sent me out to a factory and, as usual, the factory eventually offered me a permanent job. There were only three whites working in the place, the foreman, myself, and Dennis Ray Simons, who became my best friend in Hawaii. Other than that the workers were Portuguese, Japanese, and Hawaiian. My days as a racist were long over. I had learned to accept people for what they were, and most of these men were good workers and decent people.

Eventually I was offered an opportunity to work the graveyard shift, all night, and I jumped at it. I worked from midnight to 8 A.M., and as soon as I got off I grabbed my surfboard and headed for Waikiki to catch the small waves. One day in particular I remember lying on the beach, listening to the ocean, watching a very pretty Hawaiian girl sunning herself, and I started thinking to myself, This isn't too bad for one of the most wanted men in the country. I felt as safe as I had ever felt. For the first time since I got out I was really enjoying the freedom I had worked so hard for.

Not that I ever forgot that I was somewhat of a desperado. I continued to check the post office for my wanted poster. I always had a story ready for any situation. I protected my identification documents like they were gold. And I still laid awake some nights wondering about my boys, my parents, and my sister. Occasionally I even thought of Trestlee and the rest of them, and wondered how they managed to survive.

The first few months in Hawaii I felt a little like a flea in a dog pound: there were so many pretty women around I didn't know where to start. So I just kept meeting one woman after another, but the relationships never progressed very far. Then I met the first Jewish girl of my life, Susan Kalman.

I first saw her standing at a bus stop. She had long, glowing black hair and terrific green eyes and she was wearing a beautiful muumuu, the long flowered dress that women wear in Hawaii. I wasn't intending to take a bus anywhere, but I stopped to talk to her and ended up climbing on her bus and walking her home. We stopped for a drink and I could see she was extremely knowledgeable and intelligent. I laid my knowledge on thick. In my cell at Raiford first and later in my travels I had started learning about literature and art and music.

"It's really nice to meet someone who knows the difference between Salvatore Dali's surrealism and the wheatfields of Vincent Van Gogh," I told her. "Someone who can tell the difference between a Verdi opera and a Beethoven symphony."

She just smiled.

Three weeks later I moved out of the dormitory and into her condominium near Diamond Head. We had a good, solid relationship. She worked days as a secretary at Pearl Harbor, we spent every evening together, and I worked all night. By then I knew her whole story. She had been married to a fellow in New York City, they had one child, and they owned a small garment factory. Her husband, she said, was one of the worst sex deviates who ever lived. Among many other things, he had trained her to be the man, the aggressor, while he was the submissive one. So she could only enjoy sex if she was on top and did the man's part. He also liked to involve her in scenes with three and four people.

Eventually they sold the factory and moved to Los Angeles. She got a job as a screenwriter for one of the studios and he stayed in the

116

garment business. Eventually the whole thing got to be too much for her and—I couldn't believe it when she told me this—she had a mental breakdown and had spent almost two years in an institution.

I remembered my fruitcake from Myrtle Beach. That kind of problem I didn't need, but I couldn't believe Susan would be like that. She seemed perfectly healthy in her head.

Three months after we had moved in together, her brother showed up from New York. We went out for dinner and, when Susan left, he leaned over and said to me, "Sam, I really can't thank you enough for what you've done for my sister."

"What do you mean?" I asked.

He laughed. "She is so lovely, so radiant, so healthy and alive. You can't believe the bad shape she was in. It's just totally unbelievable the way she was then and the way she is now."

That made me feel good. It had been a long time since I had been able to do something for anybody else but myself.

"You know what love does for people," I told her brother. "She's happy with me and I'm very happy with her."

About three weeks later, it was my night off and we were in bed sleeping. All of a sudden the lights come on and someone is shaking me. The first thought that went through my mind was police, but before I could panic I realized it was only Susan. I started to relax, but then I got a good look at her. She had a glaze in her eyes, a stare I had never seen before. A stare that scared me, in fact.

"Who are you?" she said very deliberately.

"I'm Sam," I said. "Sam. Don't you know me?"

"You Aryan bastard." Her voice was low and even and very threatening. "What are you doing here?"

I knew just what was happening. "Now don't get excited. I'm Sam and I've been staying with you."

"Get out," she told me. "You don't live here and I never saw you before." There was real hatred in her voice when she spoke.

I have no idea what happened, but it was heartbreaking to see this beautiful woman break down like that. I tried to talk to her but it did absolutely no good. She just wanted me to leave, get out, pack everything and be gone.

"All right," I finally told her, "you're right, I shouldn't be here, I should go." I had been through this once before in Cleveland, and from my experience at Chattahoochee, I knew it was useless to try to reason with her. I packed my bags and went back into the Jungle.

I waited until mid-morning, then I called her. No use, she didn't know me at all. After I hung up I called her brother in New York and told him what had happened. "She doesn't want to talk to me, so there's nothing I can do but tell you." I really wanted to help, but I just could not get involved.

I moved into a really nice little apartment complex in the Jungle, three apartments upstairs, three downstairs, and two other buildings across a courtyard. It was clean, fairly new, and relatively inexpensive. I kept track of Susan through her next-door neighbor, hoping that maybe she would come around. But after a few weeks I realized that she had snapped for good. She just sat around the apartment, screaming at invisible people. She never went out at all, she even paid somebody to pick up her groceries for her. Finally her brother had to commit her again. The last I heard, she was living in her own world in a mental institution in Hawaii.

I missed her a great deal, because she was a beautiful person in every way. But once I broke up with her I started spending a lot of time with Dennis Ray Simons, and between the women he knew and the women I was meeting, there always seemed to be plenty of company. Life was turning out to be everything I hoped it would be in Hawaii.

Of course, I never for one minute forgot that I was on the run. In fact, through Dennis I started developing the perfect identity, the one that I eventually lived under in San Francisco. I had purchased a beat-up old wreck of a car from one of the Portuguese boys I worked at the factory with, because driving was the absolute only way I could get back and forth to work. It was extremely dangerous for me to drive, but I had no choice, I had to get to work. If I got stopped without a license I knew my Sam Wilson identification probably would not hold up, and there was no way I could get a driver's license myself because that required one little fingerprint. A spot of ink and the tip of a finger, not a very large thing to have so huge a meaning in someone's life.

I got a real break when Dennis lost his license and applied for a duplicate. After it arrived he found the original. He knew I was driving without a license, although he didn't know why and never asked, and offered me the original. I took it and protected it like a solid bar of gold.

We were physically very different. Dennis was bigger and heavier than I was, and so I very carefully changed the height and weight on the license. I really did a job on it, it looked absolutely perfect. Then I had it laminated in plastic so it couldn't be held up to the light and examined, and hid it under the floorboards of the old car. Now I had the first piece in a very complicated jigsaw puzzle: putting together the pieces of a fictional person's life.

After I had established myself as a good worker in the factory, the Teamsters Union showed up and started talking about organizing the workers. The management was really against it and, at first, so was I. But then I began to listen to the union organizers and many of the things they said made a lot of sense. Independently, the worker has no protection. United together, in a strong group, everything about the job could be improved. Although that's a very simple explanation, it's basically what the union movement is about.

I started talking to some of the Hawaiian and Portuguese men who had serious questions, and I was as open and honest as I could be. Finally there was an election and the union won. Unfortunately for me, the company decided to retaliate before the union could really organize within the factory.

"Due to a cutback in orders," my foreman explained to me, "there's going to be some layoffs. We're starting with the graveyard shift."

I knew exactly what that meant. Although I had some seniority, the company was going to punish me for my union activities by firing me. I got the official word a few days later.

At first I took it hard. With the exception of the police department, which I left for other reasons, it was the first time I ever was laid off. It was tough, hard work, but it was honest and at the end of the day you felt like you were a working man. I enjoyed working the machines, I enjoyed working with a good group of men, and I enjoyed getting paid every week.

At first I was really worried about getting another job. There was always the labor pool, but I liked the idea of something permanent. I tried a few large places but couldn't find anything at all. Then I realized there was no great rush for me to find work. I had a few hundred dollars saved up, a few close friends, the sun, the surf, and my freedom—everything that I wanted.

I was feeling very safe and secure. So secure, in fact, that as Sam

Wilson I decided to apply for unemployment payments. I had a social security number, I had proof that I had worked and been laid off for no fault of my own, so why not collect?

I applied and received the full amount, $60 a week, I think, for the next six months. It started out to be the best six months of my life. I would lie on the beach and think of my old buddies in Orlando walking a beat in the hot sun, or sitting in jail. Then I'd roll over and put my arm around my female companion of the moment and think how lucky I had been. Each day I felt a little more secure and a little happier. I started to forget how thin the line between freedom and captivity was, and how I couldn't afford to make the slightest mistake.

Which, of course, is precisely when I made that slight mistake.

12

I was living in a fantasy world of blondes, brunettes, sun, and ocean. The real world of cops and courts and prisons was fast disappearing. Instead of concentrating on protecting my freedom, the most important thing in my life during that period was the Japanese Karate International Center on Britannia Street.

I was already tough enough to win most fights, but I wanted to learn dexterity, balance, and some sort of grace. My instructor was a fifth-degree black belt from Yokohama named Mitzu. If there ever had been a perfect human being, here he was. He was as tough as anyone I've ever met, although small, but he was also as meek and humble and kind as anyone could possibly be. He only existed to do good for other people, although he was fully aware he could destroy any human being with just his hands. After meeting him I tried to pattern my life after this man.

I had been studying a few weeks when Mitzu brought another black belt expert to class for a demonstration. He took ten huge roofing tiles and smashed them with his fists. Right through! I was really impressed, because I've known very strong men who couldn't possibly have done that. It was much more a test of mental capability than physical strength. From the minute I saw those tiles smash, I wanted to break ten myself. I waited a few weeks and then, after karate practice one day, I went out back, piled up ten tiles just like the black belter did, and smashed down. And through! I was so proud of myself, I was just a purple belt beginner, but I was doing something black belts were doing.

After that there was no stopping me. I was smashing tiles all over the place, with my head, my elbows, my feet, my legs, and my hands. I'd buy them in school and bring them home and make my friends watch while I demonstrated.

Probably the highlight of my venture into karate came in class about three months after I had been in training. Mitzu was explaining a throw-hold and he asked me to grab him from behind and squeeze his arms to his side. I did exactly that. No matter how hard he tried, he couldn't break free. I had crushed him. He stopped the class, bowed to me three times, then said to everyone, "Sam is the toughest, strongest man I ever teach."

My head was about ten feet off the ground. At that moment I felt just about as disassociated from being on the FBI's ten most wanted list as I ever did. I wasn't John William Clouser, psychopath, wanted for armed robbery. I was Sam Wilson, strongest man in the Japanese International Karate Center.

After Susan's breakdown I mainly played with Dennis and the girls we met. We would run into female tourists in Hawaii on vacation and looking for some sort of adventure. Invariably they all had these very romantic notions and Dennis and I were happy to help them fulfill their fantasies. But I've always been a man who likes to have one woman, and the one woman I really wanted to have was a Korean girl named Kim.

Kim was a beautiful young Korean girl who had left Seoul when she got married. Her husband was a Sicilian immigrant, but he was stationed on an aircraft carrier in Southeast Asia when I met her. She lived next to me in the apartment complex and I would see her walking in or out, or getting her mail, or coming back from shopping, and I'd say hello. She was so shy she didn't even answer me for about two weeks. Finally, one day, she broke the ice and said, "Hello."

Well, with that encouragement there was no stopping me. Every time I saw her I would ask her to dinner, dancing, or at least to go to the beach for a swim with me. I never worked so hard to get to know one woman in my entire life! I guess my persistence won out, because she finally agreed to go swimming with me. After that we started to get to know each other, and maybe a month after we started dating, she made love with me.

She was wonderful. I wanted her to move in with me but she refused. She was very self-conscious about her reputation. Her father had been a military man and raised her with a very strong moral code. Even though we were sleeping together every night, she refused to speak to me in public at the apartment complex. When we met in the daylight it would be on the beach. At night she would very carefully sneak into my place. We never, never showed any affection for each other in the complex.

I fell head over heels in love with her. I wanted her to come to San Francisco with me, where she could get a divorce and we could get married.

"No, no," she kept telling me, "cannot do. Must be loyal to husband."

"Listen," I pleaded with her, "this is America, this is not Korea. You can do whatever you want."

122

She really was scared of her father. "Father can take my life. We cannot do this, always must remain loyal to husband!"

"Do you love him?" I would ask her.

"No."

"Do you love me?"

"Yes."

"So why can't you leave your husband and come with me?"

"Cannot do it."

It was so frustrating. This was the same answer I had gotten from SueEllen in Cleveland. People put their beliefs in some things I find very strange. There really is no way to understand them, the best you can do is just try to accept them. And I really did try to accept Kim as she was, for as long as I could have her. We had a wonderful, almost secret, shared romance. I spent a great deal of time just thinking about her, and how to win her, when I would have been better off concentrating on myself.

One afternoon I came back from the beach and was in my apartment changing my clothes when this huge Hawaiian comes walking into the courtyard. I had never seen him before, so I stopped changing and started watching. Sure enough, he takes a knife out of his pocket, sticks it into the locked screen door of one of the downstairs apartments, and cuts it open. Then he reaches through, opens the door, and walks in.

I couldn't believe what I was seeing in broad daylight. My mind really started racing. If I went downstairs I could probably grab him, but that would mean getting involved with the police. Fortunately, the apartment he broke into was unoccupied. I knew there was nothing in there but a bed and chest of drawers, so I decided not to do anything.

Sure enough, he came out empty-handed. Go, I thought to myself, get the hell out of there, you fuck, don't go near any other apartments. I really liked all the other people living in the place and I knew I couldn't just stand by and let anyone I knew get robbed. Go, I thought again, just get out of here.

He didn't go. Instead he walked directly to the apartment of a very attractive single girl named Valerie. Valerie didn't do much of anything except play all night and sleep most of the day. I was pretty sure she was in the apartment.

He pulled out his knife again and cut a hole in the screen. I knew exactly what could happen if she woke up, found him there, panicked, and screamed. A scared man with a knife can be very dangerous.

If I could scare him off and let him get away, no harm would be done. So I went down the rear staircase and, instead of coming up directly behind him, I came up on the side. That left him a way to get out and make his getaway down the street.

"Hey, you, get away from that door! Get the hell outta here, you sonofabitch!" I hollered.

Instead of running, he turned on me with the knife. It was a small penknife, but I knew it could do some real damage. He came right at me, and I knew I was going to get a chance to try out my new karate knowledge. I gave him a little head fake and then gave him my ten-tile smash right on his arm. The knife went flying onto the sidewalk. Then I slugged him right in the temple and he dropped smack on the ground and started rolling around moaning in pain. I kicked the knife away, grabbed him by the wrist, and put an armlock on him.

By now everyone in the complex has heard the fighting and moaning and they come running out. Pierre, a good friend living in one of the other apartments, was the first person down.

"I caught him trying to break into Valerie's apartment," I said.

"Don't worry, just hold him," Pierre yelled as he started running out to the street. "I'll get the police."

Now I was holding the guy down by standing on his head. I was afraid to let him up because I didn't know what he was capable of doing, so I couldn't stop Pierre. I yelled after him, "Wait, let's not be too hasty," but he was already out the front gate. Don't worry, he said, he was getting the police. What he couldn't know was that I had more to worry about from the police than the stupid burglar did.

It seemed only a matter of seconds before two of Honolulu's finest showed up. They handcuffed the burglar, examined the torn screen, and knocked on the door. Valerie slowly walked out, wearing her best towel.

"Pardon me," one of the cops asked, pushing the burglar forward. "Do you know this man?"

"No. I've never seen him in my life."

They pointed to me. "Do you know this man?"

"Sure, he lives upstairs."

They asked her if she had heard any strange noises.

"Oh, yes," she said, "I heard someone fooling around at the front door. But I was in bed and I didn't have any clothes on and I was scared. I just laid there."

Scared! All she had to do was scream or get up or make a noise,

124

anything, and this bum would have taken off. Instead she just laid there.

The police took my name and address and told me someone from the district attorney's office would be contacting me shortly. Then they left and I went upstairs and poured myself a long drink. I understood exactly what was going to happen. I was going to be subpoenaed and brought to court to testify. And when that happened my past was going to be checked. The police were going to find out that Sam Wilson didn't exist, and that would be the end of freedom for Jack Clouser.

If it wasn't for Kim I would have packed my bags and been out of that place in a matter of hours. But I was really in love with her and I just couldn't bring myself to leave. I'll wait, I told myself, until they actually subpoena me, and then I'll leave. From my days as a policeman I knew they weren't going to do any checking until the case came up.

And so I waited. Each week I'd call the police department to find out what was happening in the case. For three weeks nothing happened. My bags were packed and sitting in my closet, I was ready to leave on just about two minutes' notice. The sun didn't seem quite as warm, the waves weren't as high, and my feelings for this lovely little Korean girl just didn't seem as strong. I was scared again. I had been rudely reminded who I was and what I was doing.

Then I got a real break. There is racism in Hawaii, but it is the reverse of the mainland. In Hawaii the nonwhites are the leading citizens and the whites are discriminated against. There's no doubt in my mind that if the burglar had been white he would have gotten the works. But he was Hawaiian, and he was well known to the police as a petty thief who never hurt anyone. So instead of charging him with burglary he was charged with disorderly conduct and public drunkenness and given a thirty-day sentence. Thank God for plea bargaining.

When I heard the news it felt like a thousand-pound weight had been lifted off my shoulders. There would be no trial, I wouldn't have to testify, no one would be checking on me. I could stay in the complex at least a few more months, until the end of the year. I couldn't wait for Kim to get home so I could share my happiness with her. I started cooking a big Hawaiian dinner for us. We were going to have some wonderful celebration.

125

It didn't work that way at all.

Late in the afternoon there was a knock on the door. I looked out and, Jesus, there was her Italian husband standing there with a big broad smile on his face. I immediately recognized him from photographs Kim had shown me. I was almost speechless, but I did my best to hide my surprise.

"Excuse me," he started, "do you happen to know the Korean girl who lives next door?"

I nodded. "We pass by and say hello. Why?" I tried to be neighborly-protective, but not lover-protective.

"I'm her husband and I just got back from overseas. I wanna surprise her, but I can't find her. You wouldn't happen to know where she is, would you?"

I shook my head. "No idea."

"Do you know where the landlady is so I can get the keys to the place?"

I pointed out her apartment, and he left.

As soon as I closed the door I was out the back. I jumped over a big fence, out through a neighbor's yard, and ran all the way to the hotel where Kim was working as a hostess. I walked right into the place and said as plainly as I could, "Your husband's home."

The look on her face was just what mine must have been when I went to the door and discovered him standing there. A combination of surprise and great unhappiness. She took the rest of the afternoon off and we walked along the beach together.

"You must make me one promise," she said. "No matter what happen, you must not interfere. You must forget us. It's over."

"But I can't—" I started to argue.

She leaned forward on her toes and kissed me. "No. No matter what happen, you cannot interfere." Then she kissed me one more time, turned, and walked down the beach toward the apartment complex.

I walked the other way. I didn't want to be there when she first saw him. I just walked up and down the beach for a few hours, thinking, worrying, wondering. The first thing I heard when I walked into my apartment were the sounds of the two of them making love. The walls were very thin and almost every sound carried into the next apartment. I really got pissed and started storming around my own apartment, making noises of my own. It was strange, this Italian was making love to his wife and I was getting upset!

For the first few days he was home, all I heard were love sounds. It almost seemed to me they never got out of bed, and it was driving me crazy. But after he got tired of lovemaking he started getting tough with her. I could hear him screaming, "You don't love me! Who's your boy friend? Who have you been having as a lover since I've been gone?" *Wham!* I'd hear him smashing her against the wall. I'd hear her crying, and there was absolutely nothing I could do about it.

This went on for weeks, him balling her, and then beating her. I would see her in the courtyard and she'd be bruised, but she just walked right by me. I couldn't stand it, but there was nothing I could do about it. She made me promise not to interfere. So I had no choice but to stay out of my apartment as much as possible. Being there and listening was torture, worse even than being in prison.

The year 1966 was ending, and it was worry time again. I knew Sam Wilson's time was about to run out, but I didn't want to leave Hawaii. This really is paradise, I thought, I want to stay. So, slowly, I was convincing myself I could afford to stay one more year on the island. All I needed was a new identity and a new place to live. After almost three years on the run, getting both didn't seem too difficult. It's done, I decided, I'm staying right here in Hawaii. Then I set out to celebrate the new year, a celebration that almost ended my stay in Hawaii.

About ten of us decided to have a New Year's Eve beach party. I started drinking about eight o'clock and really got into it. The more I drank, the more I thought about Kim, so the more I drank. We had wine and good hard liquor. Unfortunately, we also had hundreds of little firecrackers. We started lighting them and throwing them around the beach and really bothering people. We weren't paying any attention to anybody.

I took two firecrackers and lit them and looked up to throw them—and there stood a big man in a big blue uniform. I quickly pushed the firecrackers into the sand, smothering the fuse.

"Don't you know it's illegal to throw firecrackers on the beach?" the policeman said.

If I had stood up I would have fallen right on my face. He had come on me so quick, and I was so drunk, I really didn't have too much time to even remember what my story was. "Um, well, you see—" All my friends had become quiet and were just sitting there listening and watching.

"What's your name?"

After all I had gone through, after all the narrow escapes I had made, the police were going to make me for throwing goddam firecrackers!

I thought as quickly as I could in my condition. All I had on was a bathing suit, a pair of shower shoes, and a T-shirt. Not one bit of identification, therefore nothing for him to check. I took my gamble: out of thin air I made up a name.

"George Diamond," I told him. I was hoping that none of the people I was with would laugh, or make a wiseass comment, or call me by my real-fake name, Sam Wilson.

"Where do you live, Mr. Diamond?" the cop asked. It was obvious he was going through the motions. I really had to pray he wasn't short on arrests for his monthly quota. I made up an address miles down the beach. He wrote it down.

"Do you have any identification with you?"

Now I was into my story and the answers came a little easier. "Nothing," I answered in as apologetic a tone as I could muster. "Everything's down in my apartment."

"I'm afraid I'm going to have to ask you to come in with me until we can identify you."

I opened my mouth to beg, to plead, anything, but my friends beat me to it. Don't take him in, they said, give him a chance, it's New Year's Eve, we can identify him. As a group they started pleading my case, and I could see the cop starting to waver.

I decided to take the offense. "Instead of taking me in," I asked, "why don't you and me take a walk down the beach to my place? I'll show you my identification and everything'll be O.K. That way you won't have to spend all night at the station booking me and I won't have to stay in the cage all night."

When I started using words like "cage," he started getting interested.

"Where'd you pick that language up?"

"I used to be a policeman," I said honestly. "Back in Cleveland," I finished dishonestly.

"Why'd you leave the force?" I wasn't sure if he was curious or questioning.

"My damn patrol sergeant. We just never got along and he pretty much made sure I'd never make sergeant. There didn't seem any reason to stay."

As soon as I told him about my problems with my sergeant, he started identifying with me, as many policemen will do. "I know," he agreed, "I know." He looked around at all my friends. "O.K., since this is New Year's Eve, I'll just make a notation of this. If any reoccurrence of this type of behavior occurs, then we'll have to come out and charge you."

"Thank you very much, officer," I told him, and I meant it. "Have a very happy new year." I watched him every step as he walked off the beach.

One of my friends waited until he was long gone, then asked, "What the hell was that George Diamond routine?"

This time I had my old story prepared. "I've got traffic warrants out on my car, so I had to give him another name."

"Good thinking, man," another one said, "good thinking."

It really was. And it was a wonderful New Year's Eve celebration. After those few moments I had a lot to be happy about.

13 The two close calls convinced me I had to start working on better identification. Sam Wilson was very flimsy to start with, and he would never hold up under any examination. The Dennis Ray Simons driver's license was a good start on another new life. The fact that Hawaii issued lifetime licenses at that point, rather than ones that expired and had to be renewed, made it invaluable. But I knew what I really needed was a social security card of my own.

One of the people I had become friendly with was about twenty years old and looked something like me. After I had known him about eight months—this was the spring of 1967—I decided to take a chance with him. I invited him out to dinner and told him the then-true story of my life.

"Sam Wilson is not my real name," I began. "I'm living a lie. When I lived on the mainland I had the single most horrible wife that ever lived. Being as young as you are, you can't understand it, but the pressure just kept building up to where I couldn't take it."

"I understand," he said seriously.

"So one day I just disappeared off the face of the earth and started a new life," I continued. "But because I don't have a real identity, at the end of every year or two, I have to move somewhere else and start all over again."

"I understand," he said again.

"If you've got the balls to do me a favor, you could make it possible for me to settle in one place and live a life like anyone else. It's really not even dangerous, just very important."

"What do you want me to do, Sam?" he asked.

I felt my heart start beating faster. "I want you to go down to the social security office and register as Dennis Ray Simons. Tell them you're a student and you never had a card because you never worked. I'll give you all the information you need."

He shrugged. "I'll do it for you, Sam, but why can't you do something like that yourself?"

The answer was easy. "I'm more than ten years older than you are. If a man my age walked into the office and applied for a new card, they'd have to start asking questions like 'How come you never applied before? Where have you worked? Can you prove it?' Stuff like that. You're young, it's really possible someone your age never had a card before."

"It doesn't sound too difficult," he said. "O.K., I'll do it."

We sat down and went to work. I made a long list of the information I thought he might need, my mother's maiden name, father's date of birth, the city I was born in, brothers and sisters. When it came to date of birth I gave him the date on the driver's license, only ten years younger. That way, if anyone ever inspected the driver's license and social security registration, they might just assume the different dates were caused by a typographical error.

My young partner memorized all the data I gave him and went down to register for me. Within two weeks I had my own social security card, a number issued to me as Dennis Ray Simons. I had created an identity for a person that didn't exist, and put him on the computers of America. The real Dennis Simons would never have to know, because my number was different than his, and the world is certainly big enough for two Dennis Ray Simonses.

When the card came I put it with the driver's license and hid both of them away. There was no way I could start my perfect identification in Hawaii because too many people already knew me as Sam Wilson.

I was pretty happy, not working too hard, and when I was offered a job as a dishwasher I took it. I've never been afraid of rough work and it paid pretty good. What was important was that none of the people who worked there knew me by any name except Sam. So when I went in I invented a new last name and a very fictitious social security number. I got my check every week, with a percentage taken out for social security. I never could guess what happened to the money being taken out. But I knew the government wouldn't check up on me until the end of 1967, so I had about eight months to really enjoy Hawaii.

My neighbor Pierre and his old roommate Lonnie decided to move in with me and we took a place right at the foot of beautiful Diamond Head. I was living two completely different lives. To everyone who knew me I was Sam, the happy-go-lucky mainlander. I started painting and writing poetry again. Almost every night I'd sit out on Diamond Head and paint abstracts or write poetry, or even just sit up there and contemplate, meditate, and procrastinate. Sam Wilson had a marvelous life.

John William Clouser was not so fortunate. There were constant reminders about how close I was to the reality of a six-by-six cell in Florida. My wanted poster still hung in the local post office. Most of

THE FBI'S TEN MOST WANTED FUGITIVES

SEPTEMBER 4, 1970

BENJAMIN HOSKINS PADDOCK, also known as: Perry Archer, Leo Genstein, Ben H. Paddock, Jr., "Big Daddy," "Chrome-dome," "Old Baldy."
W; born 11-1-26; 6'4"; 245 lbs; large bld; blond hair, balding (head may be shaved); gr or grn eyes; med comp; occ - auto mech, electrician, promoter, sales-man, serv sta worker. Wanted by FBI as ESCAPED FEDERAL PRISONER.
IDENTIFICATION ORDER #-4261
FBI#-4 530 829
FBI TOP TEN FUGITIVE

```
LM
LAM
20 L 9 R 000 18
M 1 R 000 12
```

rt ring

- - - - -

BYRON JAMES RICE, also known as: George Brent, B. J. Martin, James Byron Rice, Al Thomas, Frank Thomas.
W; born 5-17-36; 5'9"; 180-190 lbs; hvy bld; brn hair; bl eyes; med comp; occ - carpenter, janitor, lab, maintenance man, security guard, stockroom clk. Wanted by FBI for UNLAWFUL FLIGHT TO AVOID PROSECUTION (Conspiracy, Armed Robbery, Murder).
IDENTIFICATION ORDER #-4140
FBI#-689 314 F
FBI TOP TEN FUGITIVE

```
MLM
MMM
18 M 1 R 000 6
L 1 R OII 5
```

rt middle

- - - - -

JOHN WILLIAM CLOUSER, also known as: Jack Clauser, John William Clauser, Chuck A. Williams.
W; born 3-29-32; 5'9"; 175-200 lbs; stky bld; blond hair, may be dyed blk; bl eyes; rdy comp; occ - clerical worker, stock clerk. Wanted by FBI for INTERSTATE TRANSPORTATION OF STOLEN MOTOR VEHICLE.
IDENTIFICATION ORDER #-3837
FBI#-229 125 C
FBI TOP TEN FUGITIVE

```
MML
MMM
25 L 1 R 000 8
L 1 U 000 14
```

rt index

- - - - -

MARIE DEAN ARRINGTON, also known as: Louise Marie Arrington, Lola Jones Brown, Marie Swilley Dean, Dorothy Everett.
N; born 8-16-33; 5'2"; 119-126 lbs; sm bld; blk hair (usually wears wig); brn eyes; dk comp; occ - cook, domestic maid, migratory farm worker. Wanted by FBI for UNLAWFUL FLIGHT TO AVOID CONFINEMENT (Murder and Manslaughter).
IDENTIFICATION ORDER #-4267
FBI#-219 380 C
FBI TOP TEN FUGITIVE

```
6 2 U 9
2 tUr
```

rt index

- - - - -

CHARLES LEE HERRON, also known as: Lee Jones.
N; born 4-21-37 (?); 5'7" - 5'8"; 145-150 lbs; sldr bld; blk hair; brn eyes; dk comp; occ - clerk. Wanted by FBI for UNLAWFUL FLIGHT TO AVOID PROSECU-TION (Murder; Assault with Intent to Commit Murder).
IDENTIFICATION ORDER #-4163
FBI#-313 926 G
FBI TOP TEN FUGITIVE

```
M
MM
13 O 29 W 000 10
I 18 U OOI 14
```

lt thumb

- - - - -

HUBERT GEROID BROWN, also known as: Hubert Giroid Brown, Hubert Gerard Brown, H. Rap Brown, Rap Brown, Rap H. Brown, H. Robert Hall.
N; born 10-4-43; 6'3"; 180-185 lbs; med bld; blk hair; brn eyes; dk comp. Wanted by FBI for UNLAWFUL INTERSTATE FLIGHT TO AVOID PROSECUTION (Arson, Inciting To Riot, Failure To Appear).
IDENTIFICATION ORDER #-4368
FBI#-11 867 F
FBI TOP TEN FUGITIVE

```
12 12 aU 000 13 Ref:
4 aM OMM
```

lt middl

- - - - -

TAYLOR MORRIS TEAFORD, also known as: Morris Teaford, Taylor Melvin Teaford.
Ind; born 6-18-35; 5'11" - 6'0"; 170-175 lbs; med bld (muscular); blk hair; brn-haz eyes; lt brn comp; occ - lab (lumber-logging), rancher. Wanted by FBI for UNLAWFUL FLIGHT TO AVOID PROSECUTION (Murder and Assault to Commit Murder).
IDENTIFICATION ORDER #-4185
FBI#-806 823 B
FBI TOP TEN FUGITIVE

```
7 S 1 A--a Ref: T--t U--
S 1 A--a    A--a At
```

lt ind

- - - - -

WARREN DAVID REDDOCK, also known as: Doctor John R. McCann, Harvey William Rosenzweig, "Smokey" Reddock.
W; born 11-28-26; 5'8 1/2"; 150 lbs; med bld; brn hair; bl eyes; med comp; occ - accountant, machinist, oil field worker, typist, waiter. Wanted by FBI for UNLAWFUL FLIGHT TO AVOID PROSECUTION (Murder).
IDENTIFICATION ORDER #-4240
FBI#-491 649 B
FBI TOP TEN FUGITIVE

```
20 M  1 R OIO 16 Ref:
M 25 R OIO 14
```

rt midd

- - - - -

DAVID SYLVAN FINE

W; born 3-18-52 (?); 5'5"; 140 lbs; med bld; dk brn hair; brn eyes; med comp. Wanted by Federal Bureau of Investigation for SABOTAGE; DESTRUCTION OF GOVERNMENT PROPERTY; CONSPIRACY.
IDENTIFICATION ORDER #-4398
FBI#-506 562 H
FBI TOP TEN FUGITIVE

NO FINGERPRIN
AVAILABLE

- - - - -

KARLETON LEWIS ARMSTRONG, also known as: Karl Armstrong, George Reed.
W; born 10-15-46; 6'2"; 185 lbs; med bld; brn hair; brn eyes; med comp; occ - assembly line worker, mach, railroad switchman, security guard. Wanted by Federal Bureau of Investigation for SABOTAGE; DESTRUCTION OF GOVERNMENT PROPERTY; CONSPIRACY.
IDENTIFICATION ORDER #-4397
FBI#-506 561 H
FBI TOP TEN FUGITIVE

```
LM
ML
19 M 17 W IOO
L  3 W 000
```

rt litt

the other people who had been on the ten most wanted list when I first got on had long since disappeared, and I was moving toward the head of my infamous class. I was well on the way toward becoming the single most wanted man in America. Now, for the first time, political people started appearing on the list. Each time I saw a new face, I read the poster carefully. We were fellow sufferers, and I thought about the other people. I knew how justice had not been served in my case, and I honestly wondered how many other "innocent" people had their faces pinned in the post office.

Television also helped remind me that the FBI was as close as my first mistake. Each Sunday Efrem Zimbalist, Jr., played an FBI agent on the television program "The FBI," and if there was any doubt that Hoover and his giant organization were still actively looking for me, Zimbalist provided real proof. After each show, he would stand next to a poster of the wanted man of the week. I remember sitting in an easy chair and watching as my own photograph popped up on the screen.

"This man is an escaped psychopath," Zimbalist said, or something very similar. "He's a judo expert, an expert marksman, and extremely dangerous."

I didn't know who to get more angry at, an actor reading his lines, or Hoover.

Every once in awhile the newspapers would be a good stimulant also. At one point the FBI sent a story to newspapers telling them that I was a fanatical football fan, and advising pro football fans all over the country to look for me at Sunday's pro games. "Clouser is known to go to great lengths to attend pro football games," the story said. How they figured that out, I didn't know, but it simply wasn't true.

One Sunday morning when I was living with Pierre and Lonnie I got up and came downstairs. They'd already had their breakfast and were reading the *Honolulu Advertiser-Star*. One of them had opened the Sunday magazine section to a story on the top ten most wanted. There, staring me right in the face, was my own picture.

I sat down and looked at it, stared at it, took it in. First Lonnie, then Pierre caught my expression. They both laughed.

"Don't worry, Sam," Pierre laughed. "Your picture's not there, we've already checked."

"Ha, ha, ha! Thanks a lot, you guys," I joked as best I could. "Nice to know you think I'm that kind of guy." And they laughed and I laughed and inside my stomach was doing flips. I couldn't believe my roommates didn't recognize me. And I wasn't even wearing a disguise.

Another day, I was walking along the section of the beach where the muscle builders hung out. I look up and there, fifteen yards away and walking directly toward me, is my first wife's godfather. It was as if a lightning bolt had struck me. I had sat in Judy's father's restaurant in Knoxville dozens of times with this man, eating and drinking coffee.

I dropped onto the sand and started gazing out into the ocean. He walked right past me, looked at me, and didn't show any sign of recognition. I was amazed, but I realized later that when I was at the University of Tennessee I was a 145-pound skinny-assed weakling, and now I was 200 pounds of muscle, heavily tattooed, and had long blond hair.

The rest of the day I was a nervous wreck. In my whole experience as a fugitive, this was the very first time I had accidentally bumped into someone from my past. It was a possibility I never thought about, and one about which I could take no precautions. I just had to stay always alert, never relax, because I never knew who or what was waiting down the beach.

The year seemed to speed by incredibly fast. Lonnie moved out and a man named John Curry moved in and we quickly became very close friends. I took a week's trip to the outer islands and learned a great deal about Hawaii. I fell in and out of affairs with about four different women. And I remembered to keep my attention where it belonged, on keeping me free!

The old strain was starting to come back. The constant thoughts and fears. Is he a cop? What's happening over there? Have a story. Day after day the same problems, without any relief. At first the combination of my art and karate gave me some sort of outlet for my frustrations, but after awhile even they were not enough. I was getting ready to blow my top.

I broke one night at the Miramar Hotel with a Dutch girl I was dating named Katie. Katie had two things to recommend her, firm, huge breasts. They were the biggest breasts I had ever seen on a woman and, naturally, they made her the center of attraction. We danced a good portion of the night, then decided to have some drinks. The waiter was Hawaiian and obviously taken with Katie's breasts. As he served our drinks he smiled and asked, "Are they for real?" Then he squeezed them.

134

I looked at him. Then I stood up and smashed him right in the smile, sending him sprawling across the dance floor. It was the stupidest, most illogical thing I ever did as a fugitive.

The waiter got up and I knocked him down again. Everybody was screaming and scrambling to get out of the way. He got up for the third time, and this time I sent him flying into the orchestra, right on top of somebody's guitar. The waiter is trying to get up for a fourth time when I feel a pair of arms being wrapped around me. Whoever it was lifted me about two feet off the ground in a death lock. I tried everything I knew to break the hold, but I couldn't even get him to put me back down on the ground.

I never found out his name, but it was the bouncer, a football tackle from the University of Hawaii. He had me a full nelson just as the waiter managed to get some breath back.

"Get him," the bouncer ordered the waiter, and he went to work on my abdomen. Twenty-five or thirty punches later he reached my face and I was hurting pretty good. Finally the bouncer turned me loose, just dropping me on the floor.

There was too much going on inside for me to quit that easily. For the first time in my life on the run I really wanted to hurt somebody. Through my karate lessons I had strengthened my fingers to the point where they were really weapons. With all my strength I shot one of my fingers right for the waiter's eyeball. If I had hit him I probably would have killed him. But luckily, I was so groggy that I missed. I caught him on the corner of the eye. He screamed and dropped to the floor like an oak tree.

That left the bouncer. He saw the look in my eye and he knew I was out for blood. "Why don't you just leave," he sputtered as he backed away. "Just leave."

Two thoughts were running through my mind: The cops are coming, the cops are coming, and Jesus, I want this guy's ass real bad. I had to make a split-second decision and I did. The wrong one. I kept stalking him.

It took Katie to bring me to my senses. She stepped right in front of me and begged, "Sam, Sam, please don't. Let's go, let's get out of here."

Logic and reason returned just in time. Katie drove me to her cottage and did her best to patch me up. When I woke up the next day I began to realize what I had done. Not only had I taken the biggest chance of my fugitive life; I had reverted back to John Clouser. I had returned to the days when I solved everything with my fists, the days that I thought the strongest person was always right. What the hell have these years been for? I wondered. What have I learned? What about the painting and poetry and the music and dance? I couldn't believe that I hadn't really changed, that underneath I was still the same rough person. I was really upset.

Then there was a potential problem with the police. They could make a decent case for assault against me, if they could find me. Pierre started checking around and discovered that the bouncer had been taken to the hospital and might have suffered a slight loss of vision. More importantly, the waiter's brother was a member of Honolulu's famed Metro Squad, an elite police unit that consisted of the biggest, toughest members of the force.

"All they know about you is that your first name is Sam and that you hang out at the beach around the Surfrider," Pierre told me, "and they're looking for you."

"What charges are they putting down?" I was trying to decide whether to run or stay.

He shook his head. "No charges. They just want to take you for a ride."

No charges, terrific. A ride with the Metro Squad, not so terrific. I decided to stay in the apartment for a few days, just to allow things to cool off a little.

I spent most of my time inside trying to understand what I had done. There didn't seem to be any simple answer. I blamed my upbringing, my education, the constant tension I suffered with, the waiter, J. Edgar Hoover, the great American masculinity myth, and probably President Johnson. Finally I made a vow to myself that this fight would be the last time I ever raised my fists to hurt somebody. And it was. From that day on I took insults and abuse, and even the few times I was physically threatened, I simply got up and walked away.

Katie and I spent almost every day for the next three months together. We weren't in love, but we really liked each other. Then one day, with no warning, she told me she was leaving Hawaii and going to the Caribbean to be with an old black lover. I thought about it briefly and, for the first time in my life, I realized I was no longer a racist. The fact that she was leaving me to be with a black man didn't bother me at all.

136

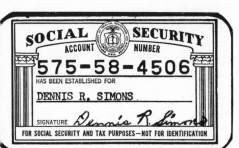

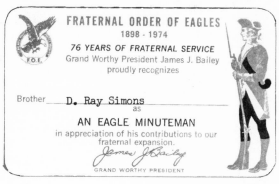

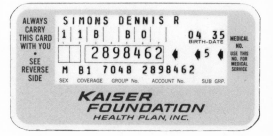

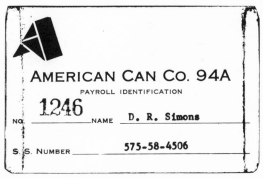

After getting a social security number in the name of Dennis Ray Simons, Clouser was able to develop a complete false identity.

Nineteen sixty-seven was coming to an end and it was time for me to seriously think about leaving. I loved Hawaii, it had become my home and I didn't want to leave, but I really had no choice. I had taken a great risk by staying on the islands a second year, and I didn't want to overtempt fate. The question was, where to move to?

The answer was San Francisco. It really interested me the short time I spent there, and it seemed as safe as anyplace on the mainland. So on September 15, 1967, I bought a $100 plane ticket, leaving me with a total life savings of $200, and left for San Francisco. The moment the plane landed, Sam Wilson ceased to exist. I decided to take the driver's license and social security card I had in the name of Dennis Ray Simons and try to parlay them into a complete identity.

It's not easy to arbitrarily change your name regularly. Unless you're concentrating all the time, you'll slip back into an old identity. Maybe you won't answer when someone calls you by your name, or maybe you'll give the wrong name during an interview, or accidentally write it down on a questionnaire, and one mistake is all it takes to start people wondering. Whenever I changed my name I would spend a few hours doing absolutely nothing but repeating the new name over and over again, until it became close to ingrained. I'd also be sure to memorize the social security number I was using, as well as the answers to all other questions I might conceivably be asked. A good memory is absolutely essential for survival as a fugitive.

My solid identification let me change my method of operation. Instead of having to go through local labor pools, I could use my Dennis Simons social security number when I applied for a job. And I could take a real job, with possibilities for advancement, because I wouldn't have to pack up and leave after one year. So for the first time in my life as a fugitive I consulted the classified want ads looking for work.

The American Can Company was hiring. I didn't know what they made, I assumed they made American cans, but I went down to apply.

About 120 people showed up and I would estimate that 85 percent were blacks and Mexicans. We all took a very tough test covering English, grammar, math, aptitude, fitting squares in triangles, and figuring other relationships. I knew I passed it pretty easily. I'm not a genius, but I'm sure no dummy, and I do have a great deal of street sense. And I did pick up a little knowledge during the two and a half years I was at the university.

138

Three days later the personnel manager called me and said, "Mr. Simons, I'm happy to inform you that you received one of the highest grades of all the applicants and we would like to offer you a job. Report to the American Can Company on Third and Twentieth for your physical!"

When I went for the physical I discovered only 26 of the 120 who took the test passed, and of those 26, 22 were white. It struck me right then that the black and Mexican kids failed not because they didn't have the same intelligence, but because most of them never had the opportunities the whites did. I was actually beginning to get a social conscience!

I was assigned to a tin-cutting machine that sliced large pieces of stamped tin into can-sized pieces, and I really liked the work. It wasn't too difficult and it wasn't creative, but for me it was fulfilling. Because I didn't have any seniority I was constantly being moved from machine to machine and even laid off for short periods of time. I didn't mind, I was learning how to work all the different equipment, and I was beginning to really enjoy San Francisco.

These were the last great days of the hippie holdouts in Haight-Ashbury. I was finding out that I had more in common with the long-haired hippies than I did with my co-workers. Most of the hippies I met really wanted to help other people and enjoy the simple things in life, and I identified with those feelings. I had bought myself a beat-up old car—now I had a registration for Dennis Ray Simons—and I continued, as always, to meet new women. There was a Russian girl I met at a skating rink. A hippie girl who worked at the post office. A co-worker. And then there was my next-door neighbor, Mrs. Lonely.

She had been married to a foreign celebrity who had divorced her and shipped her to San Francisco to keep her out of his way. As long as she stayed away from him, he supported her pretty well. I nicknamed her Mrs. Lonely because she always seemed to be by herself and looking for friendship. Actually she wasn't too bad looking, middle-aged and a decent body. Occasionally she would knock on my door and say, "Here's ten dollars, if you get me some groceries and a fifth for the two of us, you can keep the change." I still didn't have an enormous amount of money, so I did her errands. Eventually she wanted me to ball her, so I did that too.

In the middle of 1968 I got laid off for six weeks, the longest time I had been without work since my layoff in Hawaii. Because I hadn't worked at American Can long enough, I didn't get to collect unemployment. I didn't hit the labor pools because I expected to be called back after a short layoff, and considered it a payless vacation. The only problem was my payless vacation lasted too long. The rent was due and I had no money. I had no choice but to try to borrow from Mrs. Lonely.

"It's like this," I explained. "I'm really in a bad spot. I need eighty-five bucks to pay my rent. Will you loan it to me?"

A strange smile appeared on her face. She knew I was desperate, and she made me an offer. "Dennis, I'll tell you what I'm gonna do. Do you think you can make love to me for one solid hour without having a climax?"

I have a strange physical makeup. The more I drink, the more amorous I get. With enough liquor inside me I can make love for hours. "If you give me enough vodka, I think I probably can," I told her.

"If you can, I'll loan you the eighty-five."

The deal was set. If I could make love to her for one hour, on the clock, she'd loan me—not give me—the rent money. She prepared herself: she took out the wind-up alarm clock and wound it and set it for one hour. I prepared myself: I drank about three-quarters of a fifth of vodka. Then we started.

This was really work. I knew I had to have the $85 or I was in real trouble, but the thought of the challenge excited me and I started having problems right at the beginning. I tried to use an Arabic technique I had picked up in my travels. The idea is to get in a position where you lessen the tension on the sexual muscle and, at the same time, preoccupy the mind with certain thoughts to keep you from thinking about sex. Ten minutes passed, my mind was occupied trying to list the ten greatest professional golfers that ever lived. Palmer, Nicklaus, Trevino . . .

"How—how you doing?" she panted. She was having a terrific time.

"O.K.," I said. Player, Hogan, Snead, Middlecoff. Twenty minutes went by and she started moving around and I was really beginning to have problems.

"It's wonderful," she moaned. "More, do it more, more—" She moaned again.

I was busy trying to name all the states alphabetically. Montana, New Mexico, New York . . .

140

By the time we reached the three-quarter-hour mark I was really settled in. I solved my mind problem by thinking about J. Edgar Hoover. It was the greatest thing he ever did for me. With him on my mind, the possibility of enjoying sex was impossible. Now I was just riding out the end of the hour.

Mrs. Lonely was getting her $85 worth, and doing the best she could to make sure I'd lose the bet. She was hugging me and kissing me and moving around and saying every dirty word she could think of, but I had J. Edgar to keep me cool and collected.

Finally, wonderfully, the alarm clock went off. And so did I. Then I rolled over and fell on the floor and just laid there. Mrs. Lonely was as good as her word. She got right up, went to her desk, wrote out a check for $85 and an I.O.U., and handed them to me. I really earned that money. The next day the landlord showed up to pick up the rent. I endorsed the check and handed it to him. I went back to work at American Can three days later.

I thought I was pretty happy. I had a job, identification, some sort of stability, and San Francisco seemed secure. My picture was still hanging at the post office, and Efrem Zimbalist was still chasing me on Sundays, but with my mustache, goatee, and long hair I felt hidden.

I was beginning to believe that I had beaten the American system. In a society of numbers and computers, I had managed to hide out. I had created an identity where none existed, and I was using the very systems that protected society to prove my new existence. I was winning!

In fact, though, I didn't even know what real happiness could be. But I was just about to find out.

14 My life changed drastically in February, 1968, when Louis from the Can Company asked me if I wanted to take a witch to lunch. Obviously, I did. She was a white witch, a good witch, living and working in The Haight. I really didn't believe too much of anything she said until she started telling me all about myself.

"You're an Aries," she started, right on target, "and you're a man who constantly likes to be on the move." She went deeper and deeper into my personality, all of it pretty correct, and I decided to interrupt her. It was one thing to have J. Edgar Hoover and all his forces after you, quite another to have the supernatural involved.

Just then another couple Louis was friendly with, Donald and Margaret McGrew, joined us. I looked up into Margaret's eyes, and I really believed in magic. She had long black hair and beautiful features, and there was something just radiating from her, another sort of warmth and beauty. I fell in love with her right at that moment.

In my life I had met just about every type of woman, but I made a point of never messing with happily married people. There were too many single or unhappily married women around. But there was something unexplained that drew me to this woman. We never planned to meet, but we would constantly be bumping into each other in the street, or in the supermarket, or at a mutual friend's house. In fact, rather than being friends with Margy, I became good friends with her husband. We set up a little gym in a basement and lifted weights together. He had no idea what was going on in my mind, and I was doing my very best to fight it. The most guaranteed way of creating a problem is getting involved with another man's wife, and I could not afford to have any problems.

On April 2 I celebrated my fourth year of freedom. I went out drinking by myself and silently toasted my success. Four years on the run, I was doing a terrific job messing up the FBI's 147-days-on-the-top-ten-and-captured average.

As Dennis Ray Simons I had a growing group of friends, a good job at American Can, I was a member of the United Steel Workers Union and had membership cards to prove it, and, for the first time, I had a credit card! Until this point there was no way I could apply for credit of any type. An application would have meant an investigation and I couldn't stand that. So for my four years on the loose I'd paid for

142

everything in cash. I still didn't have a bank account. But when I joined the Steel Workers I received all sorts of credit, and I used it, and I never missed a payment. I was really becoming a solid citizen.

At the end of May the McGrews had a party for about forty people and I volunteered to be bartender. I spent the night mixing drinks and taking long nips for myself. By 1 A.M. I was really high. I took Margy out on the dance floor and held her very close and whispered in her ear, "I'm crazy about you. I want you with all my heart."

She pulled herself out of my arms and looked at me as if I was crazy.

I didn't give her any time to think about it. "Will you have lunch with me tomorrow?"

She answered slowly. "No, I can't. I shouldn't. I have to think."

Eventually she did agree to meet me for lunch, and for breakfast a week later, then breakfast and lunch, and finally we were meeting regularly during the day, because I was working the 3 P.M. to midnight shift at American Can and I wouldn't miss work for anything. All we did was meet and talk and get to know one another. Nothing physical happened between us. Not because I wasn't trying. I desperately wanted her; the more I got to know her, the more I was attracted to her. Not only was she one of the prettiest women I had known, she was easily one of the brightest and one of the most concerned, involved people I had ever met. She really cared about other people.

Our meetings were difficult for her. I could tell she was attracted to me, but she also felt a great loyalty to her husband. This made it tough for me too, because I really liked him. But I loved her. Eventually she told me that she married Donald as much to help him avoid the military draft as because she loved him.

Donald didn't know we were meeting, so the three of us still spent time together. One of those times came very close to being the end of my stay in San Francisco.

Donald, Margy, myself, and two other people were going on a picnic in my car. The roads in Marin County are winding, and I foolishly passed another car on a blind curve. I made it easily. Unfortunately, a woman was coming in the other direction, and when she saw me coming, she froze. If she would've swerved six inches nothing would have happened, but she just froze. I threw my car hard to the right and managed to avoid hitting her head-on. There was a short ripping sound as her left front fender tore into my right rear.

For anyone else a fender-bender accident is an inconvenience; for me it might mean the difference between freedom and prison. For an instant I started to push my foot down on the accelerator. Get away! was my first thought.

Instead I pulled my car to the side of the road. "O.K., everybody," I told the people in the car. "Pack up the beer as best you can, and if anybody's got marijuana on them, get ready to get rid of it quick if the cops come."

I started walking back toward the woman's car, and even before I got there she was screaming at me. "You jerk! You hit my new car. Are you crazy, driving like that? What are you doing?"

I did my best to calm her down. "I'm really sorry, ma'am, it was an accident. Don't worry about a thing, I've got insurance and my company'll take care of the whole thing." No police seemed to be coming. "Now sit here—"

Another car stopped in front of hers and a tall, square-shouldered man stepped out. I didn't know exactly what he wanted, until he started shaking his fist in my face.

"You'll pay, all right," he screamed, "because I saw what happened. That was your fault, I saw it all and I'm gonna testify against you. I'm going straight to the cops and you'll lose your license."

I turned from the woman. "Listen, mister. Get the hell out of here. All you're doing is making this lady nervous. Just get in your fucking car and get out. Now!"

He started backing away. "I'm going for the cops, that's where I'm going."

I did my best to ignore him, but he really had me scared. I had to get away from there before the cops came. I couldn't afford to risk losing my Hawaiian driver's license. Worse, I had no insurance. In California, to get insurance you have to have a California driver's license. And getting a California driver's license means being fingerprinted.

"We can't leave your car here," I told the woman. "I'm going to drive down the road and call the police and a tow truck. I'll be back in a little while."

I had absolutely no intention of ever coming back. I just couldn't risk it. She had my license plate number written down, so there was no avoiding the consequences of the accident, but I had to clean out my car before the police started inspecting it.

We made it about two miles before my busted fender cut through

144

the tire and flattened it. Donald and I and our friend Roy jumped out and we all pushed and pulled at the metal, but we couldn't budge it. We weren't driving any further.

"Here's the plan," I told my passengers. "Get everything out of the car and throw it over the cliff. I mean everything!"

It would have made a funny scene, if I wasn't so scared. Everybody emptying bottles of wine and beer, and shaking blankets out, watching the marijuana drift down into the sea. We're shaking and throwing and I look down the road and see a motorcycle cop coming toward us. Inside I prepared myself for still another encounter with the police department.

He looked tough as he climbed off the motorcycle, but he turned out to be the nicest, most polite cop I ever met in my life. "What happened down there?" he asked.

I grimaced. "We had a little accident. I passed blind and struck the lady. It was my fault and I was trying to get to a telephone to call you, but my tire went flat."

"Don't you know there's no phone booths at all this way?"

I most certainly did, I'd been down this road a dozen times, and that is precisely why I picked this direction. "No, officer, this is my first trip this way. I just got to California from out of the state." I could tell my passengers were listening to this strange conversation carefully.

"Can I see your license?"

"Certainly." I took out my forged and sealed Hawaiian license and handed it to him. He examined it carefully, both sides, then he started writing out the accident report. He believed it! I relaxed.

"May I have your California address, please?"

I gave it to him with pleasure. I had to give him the correct address because it was on my registration, and the registration was completely legitimate. You don't need a fingerprint to register a car.

In very official fashion the officer said, "All right, I'll file this report and you'll be notified by mail what has to be done."

"Fine," I said, "and would you do me a favor, officer? Call me a wrecker so I can have him pull the fender off my tire so I can change it."

He agreed.

I stuck out my hand. "Thank you, officer, you've been most polite and most courteous."

He climbed on his motorcycle and drove off, leaving us safely alone. The wrecker showed up, we changed the tire, and we had one wonderful picnic. We had no marijuana left—I didn't mind as I only smoked on occasion—but we did have plenty of wine and beer stashed away. We finished every drop of it. I was feeling very confident. My identification had passed inspection. I was a person. I was Dennis Ray Simons!

Two weeks later, the beginning of June, I received a summons in the mail. Basically it said that the accident was my fault and the state required that I post a bond of $37.50 and show up in court later that month. I called the motor vehicle bureau and asked, "If I send my check for $37.50 and choose not to appear in court, will anything else happen?"

The woman on the other end of the phone really didn't want to answer the question, but she finally admitted that, as long as I didn't contest the ticket, there would be no repercussions.

"No court appearances, no arrest, no nothing?"

"No," she reluctantly agreed, "nothing."

I went directly to the post office, bought a money order for $37.50, and mailed it in. Now it was beginning to look like I might get away really clean from the accident. Then I got another letter from the state of California, this one informing me that since their records showed I had no insurance coverage, I was personally liable for damages to the other car amounting to $360.

There was no way I could pay that bill. I just didn't have that kind of money saved up. Besides, I'd seen the other car and there was absolutely not $360 worth of damages. No way. So I filled out the highway patrol forms admitting the accident was my fault, and then explaining I couldn't pay the damages. I wasn't sure what would happen next. The case, I hoped, was closed.

I was dangerously wrong. By the end of June California informed me that my license was hereby suspended for two years. Worse, the state wanted me to surrender the license itself. California wanted me to give up my identity.

I didn't know what to do. The FBI was something I could deal with. It consisted of flesh-and-blood agents, people you can figure about. The computerized bureaucracy was something else. I knew I couldn't afford to give up Dennis Ray Simons's license. It was just too valuable. Anywhere except the state of California it was still perfectly good, and I didn't know how much longer I was going to be staying in San Francisco. So I decided to put my letter into the red tape. Confuse the state, if possible. I wrote a letter saying I was no longer a California resident, and therefore I will not be driving in California, and so I will not surrender my license. I put that letter inside a larger envelope and sent it to a friend in New York to be mailed—and postmarked—from there.

Next, since Dennis Ray Simons's registration was no longer any good in California, I sold the car. To myself. Actually, to another new myself, Frank Ryan. It was very simple. I went to the motor vehicle bureau and signed the car title over to a fictitious name, Frank Ryan, and paid the transfer fee. Within three weeks Marin County mailed the new title to me. That way, as far as the state of California was concerned, the car was still legally registered in the state.

Finally, to cover myself completely, I moved. That might seem like a major solution to a minor problem, but I just couldn't afford to take the chance on anyone checking. I was depending on the computer system to get so involved in red tape that nobody would ever figure out what I had done. I just had to hope, for example, that nobody realized that the car was now registered to an individual who had no California driver's license, had never paid any state tax, or federal tax if they wanted to check that, who didn't work or pay social security, had no bank accounts and didn't even have a library card. I figured the mass of documents the state had to work with would simply overwhelm them and Frank Ryan would be swallowed up into the wires and circuits, never to appear again.

But just in case that didn't happen, I changed apartments and left no forwarding address.

I used the same old story on my friends: I owed $300 and couldn't pay it. They all accepted it without question.

The only problem that left me with was that I couldn't drive the car. It was just too dangerous to risk. But driving turned out not to be necessary. All of a sudden I found myself someone to drive for me. Margy.

Our breakfasts and lunches together had turned into whole mornings and finally, at the end of June, she came to my apartment and we made love for the first time. It was wonderful, beautiful, and marvelous. I had made love to many women in my life, but I very rarely had any deep feelings about them. With Margy I really felt great joy and happiness.

She must have felt the same way; a few days later she told her

147

husband she was leaving him and moved in with me on 17th Street. At first her husband was furious, and I was worried about what he might do, but when he found out that I was the other man he calmed down and accepted her decision. Impossible as it may seem, we all managed to stay friends.

Dennis Ray Simons was becoming a solid citizen. I had so much identification I could have stood up under any examination in the world. I paid my income tax and even got a refund. I even went so far as to open a joint bank account with Margy, although I made a careful point of always keeping a few hundred dollars hidden in the apartment, with my Hawaiian identification, just in case I had to move quickly again.

No one suspected anything. I was meeting people all the time—the people Margy and I socialized with, the people I worked with, the people I played golf with, the people in the Fraternal Order of Eagles, who initiated me as a member. At times I would wonder, If I can keep this secret, what secrets are these other people hiding? What is their past? I was amazed to think how little anyone actually knows about his friends. These were good people, friends, people I loved, and yet they knew absolutely nothing about the real life I was hiding from them.

The only reminders I had were the occasional newspaper and magazine stories, Efrem Zimbalist each Sunday, and my poster hanging in the post office. The FBI had actually split up the list into two parts, one for common criminals, like myself, and the other for political criminals, like Angela Davis and Bernadette Dohrn. I was heading right for the top of my list. One by one I watched familiar faces disappear from the walls.

I was constantly wary, but there were brief moments when I was able to relax. I had really become Dennis Ray Simons in being as well as in name, so I didn't have to be consciously aware of every move I made or everything I said. My running had come to a walk.

Before my arrest in Orlando, money was the most important thing in the world to me; money and the material things it could buy. All I wanted was a big Cadillac, a diamond ring, good clothes, a big television set. Now my freedom was really the only thing that mattered. I didn't want to own anything. I just wanted to eat and drink and laugh and have a woman to love me and love her back.

With Margy I had all those things. She taught me things I never knew. She dragged me to the opera but went to the ball games too, encouraged my painting, read my poems, and laughed at my jokes. The next year was the happiest one of my entire life.

Little by little we learned about each other. Margy had degrees from two colleges and was studying for a doctorate. I was amazed. I told her I was an ex-cop. She was amazed. Politically, she was a strong socialist, she really believed everybody should share what they have. She explained to me how she believed the working people in America were being given less than they deserved and showed me how really important the union movement was.

But as strong as she was politically, she was softer emotionally. *Life* magazine once did a story on the starving children of Africa, and I remember she read it and sat in our big easy chair for three hours, crying. She was so tender that through her I lost all thoughts of revenge and hatred for the people in Orlando who had sent me to prison unjustly. I didn't care about Jim Russ or Hoover or Trestlee. Margy and my lost sons, they were the people in the world who mattered.

Margy never asked me too much about my past and I didn't volunteer. I told her I'd left the force and bummed my way around the country, discovering what life was like. I spoke in very idealistic terms and until much later we never got into any specifics about my past life.

I had absolutely no problem with the police for an entire year. But on July 4, 1969, I ran into a minor problem for anyone else, a potential disaster for me. Independence Day almost proved to be the end of my independence.

Margy and I and some friends from American Can were invited to a party in Burlingame, a small city outside San Francisco. Among the people there was Gary Schaeffel, a divorced man who was dating, believe it or not, an ex-sergeant in the WACs. She'd been married for six years to an impotent lieutenant, and the way Gary explained it, now she was trying to make up for lost time.

The party was fun and we all drank too much and we were standing on the back balcony overlooking a huge field. Gary had some fireworks and he handed me a cherry bomb.

"Throw it out there," he said as he lit it.

I did exactly that. Unfortunately, it landed in the dry grass. Immediately flames started shooting in every direction. Everyone there knew how dangerous a wild grass fire could be in a dry, residential area. What had been a silly joke had become a potential disaster, far worse than anything I had ever been involved in before.

We all went tearing out of the house and down the hill. Margy was the first person down and she was trying to smother the flames with a blanket she'd grabbed. We were right behind her, crazy people, running all around, kicking up dirt, using shirts to beat down the flames, throwing as much water out the window as possible. But it didn't seem to do any good. The fire kept spreading.

Margy was dashing from one area to another, shouting orders, flinging her blanket, oblivious of her own safety. Finally she lost her footing and slipped, right into the burning grass. Her skin just blistered right up, but we managed to get her up and out before she was seriously hurt.

I was fighting the fire like a crazy man. Normally the stupid things I did only threatened my own safety, but this fire was a danger to everyone in the area. I tried as best I could, but I wasn't making any more progress than anyone else in beating down the flames. "Call the fire department," I screamed. "Somebody call the fire department!"

They must have already done it, because fire trucks were on the scene within minutes. It took them a decent period to get the fire under control, and, by the time they did, it had burned close to a whole acre. With the exception of Margy, who wasn't seriously hurt, no one was injured and no buildings or homes were damaged. We were just very, very lucky.

After the firemen came the policemen. They wanted to know what caused the fire. They started asking everyone questions and, at first, all my friends pretended to have no knowledge of the beginning. I was sick. I knew it would be just a matter of time before somebody contradicted someone else and the responsibility came around to me. The penalty wouldn't be much for starting the fire, it was a stupid accident, but an accident. It was the investigation and the chance that I would be fingerprinted that worried me.

"Where were you when the fire began?" a policeman was asking Gary.

"Did you people have any fireworks?" another was asking my friend Ed Rucker.

"What do you think happened?" a third cop asked Margy.

It was just a matter of time.

150

Suddenly there was a loud smack, and then the sound of a young child screaming. We all turned around to see a middle-aged woman smack the boy across the face a second time. She was yelling at him in a rage, "What did I tell you about these firecrackers? Huh? What did I tell you? Goddammit, I told you not to throw any more of those, didn't I? Didn't I?" She smacked him again.

The cops looked at each other and one of them walked over to the woman. I knew I was off the hook completely. I was going to let an eight-year-old take the rap for me.

I felt useless, hopeless. My own sons were just about that boy's age. But there was nothing I could do. I couldn't risk the exposure. The worst that would happen to that boy would be a juvenile report and a good punishment from his parents. My punishment from society would be a lot worse.

Margy's burns healed quickly, but her feelings didn't. She wasn't at all happy I let that little boy suffer because of something I did. She became much cooler to me and, finally, about ten days later, I decided I had to tell her the truth, at least part of it. We were sitting in the living room, not talking, and I broke it to her gently.

"Honey," I said softly, "I love you very much and I know how difficult I am sometimes. And I know how you felt last week about that little boy. But you just have to believe in me. I couldn't take the chance of being investigated by the police, because I did some things in my past that I don't want anybody knowing about. They're just better forgotten."

She was reading the newspaper, and she put it down. "What sort of things?"

I didn't answer her directly. "Do you love me?"

"You know I do."

"Then just believe me when I tell you you're better off not knowing about it." I felt really strange thinking of myself as John Clouser. That name had been out of my mind for a long time.

She didn't say anything for a few minutes. "Will you ever tell me the whole story?" she asked.

"I swear. The first time it's safe to tell you, I will." Then I leaned over and kissed her.

It was all I could say, but it wasn't really enough. After that she seemed a little distant from me, a little more independent. She had spent most of 1969 working as a union organizer in San Francisco and in August she told me she had decided to go to England with two girl friends to study political theory for a month.

I had a raging fit. We hadn't been separated a night since we moved in together. For thirteen months I hadn't slept with another woman, the first time in my adult life I'd been that faithful that long.

"If you go," I warned her, "we're finished. I won't be here when you get back." Just the thought of her breaking the tranquillity of our home and love affair made me angry. I needed her, I was dependent on her love and kindness.

I kept threatening her and warning her right up until the moment she left. One Sunday morning she and her two friends packed a Chrysler they had rented with tents, camping gear, food, everything they needed for a two-week trip across the country, and prepared to leave.

I wouldn't relent. "If you leave me, we're finished," I told her.

She was crying. "You can't mean that. I have to have my own life too, you know. And you know how much I love you."

I stood there on the porch and watched her disappear down the road. And for the first time in over a year I felt alone and insecure.

15

It seemed like an unfunny joke. The FBI was still warning the country to be on the lookout for John William Clouser, an armed and dangerous psychopath, a fanatic who had vowed "never to be taken alive." They put me in the same category as Dillinger, Clyde Barrow, and even the real Willie Sutton. In fact, I was nothing more than a blue-collar worker who was terribly lonely and depressed because the woman I loved had left me. My mind wasn't centered on being a famous fugitive and going out in a hail of gunfire. I never went near guns. All I could think about was Margy, Margy, Margy.

I decided I had to get even with her, and the best way to do that was through other women. The first person I called was the ex-WAC who had been at the Fourth of July party with Gary Schaeffel. They had stopped dating and I figured he wouldn't mind.

"Hi, I'm Dennis," I told her on the telephone. "I'm the one who threw the firecracker."

That she remembered.

"I broke up with my girl friend," I told her, "and it's a beautiful day and I'd like to come over for a drink, and then maybe we could have dinner. Whattya say?"

She said yes.

As soon as I walked in the door she put a drink in my hand. Then she said yes again. I felt both awful and good, awful because Margy couldn't have even been out of the state of California and I'm balling another woman, and good because I was balling another woman and getting even with Margy.

We drank, sunbathed, made love, ate, drank, made love, went out to dinner, danced, came home, and made love. She was incredible. Gary wasn't kidding when he said she was making up for lost time. I had as good a time as possible, but when I left the next morning I knew it was the last time I'd ever spend the night with her. She had a terrible problem: she snored worse than anybody I'd known in my life. Maybe that's why that lieutenant was impotent!

From the ex-sergeant I went wild. Over the month Margy was gone I screwed at least four other women. I also packed all her stuff up for her because I was determined she was going to leave the minute she got back. I didn't want to be dependent on anyone, and I was getting very dependent on her.

153

In September, I got a phone call. The operator asked if I would accept a collect long-distance call from New York. "No!" I practically screamed and slammed the phone down.

A few hours later I got another call. This one wasn't collect. "Hi, honey," she said in a cheery voice. "I'm stranded in New York and I have no money. I can't get back."

I was determined to be tough. "That's too bad. You shouldn't have gone off with those people and left me. What do you expect me to do?"

"Please. I want to come home."

I rubbed it in a little more, than I agreed to help her. "I'm going down to Western Union and I'm gonna wire you some money. It's a loan. Now, I've got all your stuff packed, and when you get back, I want you to get out." I sent her enough for bus fare and about ten dollars extra for food.

Four days later she called me from the Greyhound station. I looked at her, the woman I loved, and I couldn't believe it. Her legs had swollen twice regular size from being cramped in the bus. She was ragged, dirty, her backpack was torn, she just looked terrible. I put her in the car and asked, "Where do you want to go?"

"I want to go home."

Now was my real chance to get back at her. "I told you, we're finished. It's not your home any more."

She really was hurt. "Can't I just go home and take a bath and get something to eat?"

In a gesture of humanity, I agreed. We got home and I made her dinner while she just relaxed in the bathtub. Then, right in the middle of dinner, she looked at me and I looked at her and she started crying and then I started crying and we were back in each other's arms.

"Don't ever leave me again," I pleaded with her. "I just can't take it."

She tried to explain that what she was doing was important, and that it didn't mean she loved me any less because she went away for a month.

For the first time in my entire life I confessed to being unfaithful. "You broke my heart when you left me, that's why I did it." I really didn't know how she would accept what I did.

"Do you love me?" she asked.

"Yes, I love you more than anything in the world."

154

"Then it doesn't matter."

Right at that moment, with Margy in my arms, all my running had been worthwhile. I wasn't running from something, I was running to that moment. And it was worth all the years.

We had good times and not-so-good times. Margy had a son by her first marriage (Don was her second husband), and he was exactly the age my oldest son would be. He and I never really got along very well, I always felt excluded from his relationship with Margy. I asked her about it once and she explained, "Your personality dominates my son's, and I want him to learn to do things on his own initiative." That hurt me a lot, but she was right and I accepted it.

He was a very sensitive boy, and one afternoon we had an argument and he ran away. When he came back he told Margy about the fight and she packed and moved out. For three days. Then she came back and we just picked up.

She made me so very happy. For the first time in my life I was involved in a real relationship, a love affair where people loved and fought with love, and respected the other person.

I wanted to marry her, but I was afraid. Her politics were very liberal and I was the senior fugitive on the top ten list. This was during the Nixon years and every liberal suspected that Nixon was using his presidency to destroy people who disagreed with his policies. Margy disagreed loudly. I just couldn't take the chance that the FBI or the IRS or any other of Nixon's networks might start looking around and discover my not-so-forgotten past. So we lived together on and off, but we still kept separate apartments.

My life was very stable. I had created the perfect identity. I had the love of a great woman. I had a good job that I really liked. I knew I should have been comfortable, but I had a nagging feeling something was going to go wrong. I just didn't know whether my problems would come from the police, Margy, or American Can Company.

It was American Can. They lost a major contract and decided to phase out the plant I was working in. Some of the employees with more seniority were moved into another plant, but I was laid off. At first that hurt me terribly because I loved the plant. I would have been content to spend thirty years working there. I had a bunch of good friends, I loved the work, I was always busy, and I received an honest week's wage. When I was notified, my first reaction was to start

155

scrambling for another job. But then I realized I'd be getting three-quarters of my weekly take-home pay, $65 from unemployment and $31 from American Can, and decided to take some time off and just relax.

I decided to take a real, honest-to-goodness vacation, the first time I had ever done anything like that. When I saw an advertisement for a sailboat cruise from Los Angeles to Acapulco I decided to check into it. The price was $700, but I talked the owner into giving me a $400 one-way deal, which meant I'd have to fly back on my own.

Margy thought it was a wonderful idea, which shows how different she is from me. Instead of throwing a tantrum, as I did when she was leaving, she packed my suitcases, and the night before I was leaving, Thanksgiving night, she made a huge dinner party for me.

I was feeling so confident that the fact I was going back to Los Angeles, the location of my closest escape, didn't even bother me. By this time I had to assume the FBI had just about given up hope of ever finding me. As long as I'm careful, I told myself, nothing will happen.

The name of the ship was the *Regina Maria*, a handmade replica of an old clipper ship. It was magnificent and I couldn't wait to get under way.

There was only one small problem: I had to have a Mexican government tourist card to make the trip. And I couldn't get a tourist card without a birth certificate.

At first it seemed to be an insolvable problem. I again used the bluff tactics I'd picked up on the road. "A birth certificate," I said. "How the hell am I supposed to get a birth certificate? We're leaving in three days and my birth certificate is back home in North Carolina."

The clerk at the Mexican visa bureau came up with the solution. "We will accept a notarized statement of identification," he said, "but that's it!"

I hunted down a notary public and gave her the information as fast as she could type: Dennis Ray Simons, 3562 17th Street, San Francisco, employed three years at the American Can Company. She asked to see some identification and I laid thirteen almost legitimate pieces of identification on the table, everything from a social security card to my union membership.

She went through it piece by piece. "Do you have a driver's license?"

"I don't drive," I said.

We went through everything from date of birth to my mother's maiden name. She finished typing, I signed it and swore it was the truth, and I took it back to the visa bureau.

I got my visa. Now I was on my way to Acapulco.

We had twenty-seven men, including crew, and seven women aboard. And we had a ball. For five days we slowly drifted south, spending the days lying in the sun, drinking, talking, making friends. About the third day, just about the time I was getting deeply tanned, I remember wishing J. Edgar Hoover could see me right at that moment.

Our first port of call was Turtle Bay. We went ashore and found the city exactly like so many other poor towns. The people lived in real poverty, barely existing, but right in the heart of the town was a magnificent, huge church, with a golden cross and beautiful dome. I saw that church, and looked at the shanties the people lived in, and I began to understand more of what Margy meant when she talked about injustice.

A few blocks down from the church was the cantina, the whore-house. Around noon we started drinking and playing the jukebox and dancing. By two we were all pretty drunk and having a wonderful time. I walked outside to get some fresh air and this cute little Mexican girl asked, "Make love?"

Seven dollars later I walked back inside and told some of the other men that there were girls outside. They rushed right out. I went back to my tequila, the woman passengers who were drinking with us, and the music.

Pretty soon one of the prostitutes came running into the cantina, screaming, quickly followed by one of the male passengers. Sober he was a terrific person, but now he was drunk and he had a long, sharp Bowie knife in his hand. He had given the girl six dollars but couldn't perform. He wanted his money back, she didn't want to give it to him.

I'm sitting there watching this little drama unfold and thinking to myself, All this for six dollars! A few people tried to calm the guy down, but any time anyone went near him he'd take a big swipe with the knife. This was starting to get really dangerous. When somebody shouted to call the *policía*, I decided to try to help. Ending up in a Mexican jail was not much more exciting than being in a Florida jail.

I got up very slowly, Gary Cooper like, and walked over toward him. "Bobby," I said in as bored a tone as I could manage, "give me the knife, please."

157

"Nah, Dennis, I can't. I want my money back. You better stay away from me."

"Bobby, I'm not kidding. Give me the goddam knife and let's get outta here before we all end up going to jail." Without waiting for his answer I began to move in on him. He took a long, fast swipe at me with the Bowie. I leaped back and just glared at him.

"I warned you, Dennis," he said. "Now get outta the way."

I came at him again. He moved one step toward me and started sweeping down with the knife. I blocked his thrust and grabbed his arm, twisting it hard and flipping him over my shoulder. The knife went flying across the room, skidding to a harmless stop near the edge of the bar. Nobody else in the place moved.

"Come on now, Bobby," I ordered. Then I picked him up and hoisted him over my shoulder. I carried him outside and dropped him like a lead weight on the dirt. I finished my performance by walking back inside and picking up the knife. I couldn't risk carrying it myself, so I went back outside and gave it to one of the other men and told him not to give it back to Bobby under any circumstances.

There was only one other bad moment on the whole trip. My two roommates were heavy drug users. One day in La Paz they made a buy and the person they copped from told the police. The police found me, my roommates, and three crew members in a bar. I wasn't worried, I knew better than to carry drugs in a foreign country. We finally managed to convince the *policía* that these men weren't addicts, but needed the drugs for medical reasons. The police searched them and found nothing, so they had no choice but to let these men go. It's their business, I thought. I knew better than to get involved in drugs in any foreign country.

But then I went back to the ship and, for some reason, decided to check my life preserver. It was full of drugs. Pills, grass, poppers, and other things I had never seen before. I blew my gourd. If those cops had come on board and searched my cabin, I'd be sitting in a Mexican jail. I went screaming up on deck, looking for these guys. After all I had been through, if I got caught I wanted it to be because of something I messed up, not because some morons can't keep their personal things personal.

I had cooled down by the time I saw the first one. I grabbed him and held him out over the side of the ship, at least fifty feet above the waterline. He was screaming and pleading and swearing and promising.

158

"You no-good fucking bastard," I yelled. "You pack your shit and be out of my cabin in fifteen minutes or I'll kill you. I swear, I'll kill you."

He made it in ten minutes.

Eventually my roommates got in trouble again and the captain just put them off the boat in the middle of Mexico. They did some real shouting then, but nobody listened, we were all too busy enjoying ourselves.

In Acapulco the captain invited me to sail back north with the ship, as his guest. I had really become friendly with the crew and ended up spending more time with them than I did with the rest of the passengers. But I was still subject to Montezuma's Revenge and I was tired and the quality of the good was bad and I missed Margy. So I flew home, and arrived Christmas night, 1971.

My vacation was just about over. The unemployment checks had stopped coming in and my union fund was due to expire soon, so I started looking for a job. I found one as maintenance manager, janitor actually, at the local Jewish Community Center.

The day I started working I wondered what my parents would say if they knew I was working with Jewish people. They raised me as a Methodist, but I never really felt comfortable in that church. I was later introduced to Buddhism, which I liked in a philosophical way, and I enjoyed the friendship of kind gentle people.

At the Jewish Center part of my job was setting up different activities. I set up dances at the Café Shalom and learned a great deal about the Jewish people. They are really remarkable people, and their religion is much more a complete culture than just a belief. How different they were from my family.

My parents. I didn't know if they were dead or alive. I wondered about my sister. And I feared for my sons. They were being brought up by a woman whose values were worlds apart from mine. I was happy, but I would have given anything—except my precious freedom—to see them again, to talk to them, to take them to a baseball game, to go to open school night, to sign their report cards, to buy them presents, to see them playing sports.

By this time Margy knew I had been married and divorced and had children. She knew how desperately I missed my sons, and how much I loved them. "Why can't you contact them?" she would ask.

"I can't," I would tell her. "I just can't."

She didn't understand, but she accepted my word.

In the summer of 1972 one of my friends introduced me to a man named Len Uhlman, the brother of a girl he was dating. Lenny had done good time in San Quentin for armed robbery, and was free on parole. He was desperately trying to find a job, he really wanted to go straight, but as soon as any prospective employer found out he had a record he was dropped. He was just about ready to pick up a gun and start robbing, I could tell. I knew just what was going on in his head, and I really wanted to help him.

One of my friends from American Can was the personnel director at a department store, and I asked him if he needed a good man. He said he always needed good men. Then I asked Len if he was interested in working at the store.

"All you've got to do is not mention that you're an ex-con," I told him. "Make up a story about where you've been for the last few years."

We sat down and made up the story together. He was hired and did a great job. He owed me a big debt, and later he would repay it in a strange way.

Each day my life got better. Margy understood my psychological problems about women, so she never objected when I saw someone else. But I always went home to her, and I never stopped loving her for a minute. For awhile she moved out again and stayed with her son, but we spent almost all our time together, and, except for a few of my silly flings, neither of us ever really looked twice at anyone else. Finally, in the summer of 1972, she decided that she wanted to move back in with me permanently.

"I can't do that," I said, not at all easily, "because of your involvement in causes. Someday you're going to bring heat on me and, I told you, I can't stand up under a close look."

That's when she decided she loved me more than her social work. She said she would quit all her activities if we could get back together. I agreed immediately. We found a wonderful little cottage in the back yard of my close friend Jim Cornwall's larger home, and moved in. It was small, but it was home. The first real home I had known since my childhood.

About this time I fell down a flight of stairs at work—I was carrying some ceramics from the children's craft class—and hurt my knee

160

badly. I couldn't work, I could hardly walk. The insurance company offered me a cash settlement of $1,800 or an operation. I took the cash. It was the most money I had had in my hands in years, and I was surprised to discover it didn't make any difference. It could have just as easily been eighteen dollars.

Len Uhlman and I became close friends. He introduced me to his friends and family, among them Dianne Hamilton. She was a nice-looking woman. But Lenny told me that she had done time for armed robbery in a woman's prison in California and, worse, she had been under constant psychiatric care for years. Lenny had known her since they were kids, and he felt very protective toward her. "Sometimes she has a difficult time separating her fantasy from reality," he explained to me.

I thought I knew enough to stay away from women like that.

I thought wrong.

As soon as Lenny got settled and secure he started running poker games for some of the men from the neighborhood. Dianne was the hostess. She'd serve drinks and sandwiches and her salary came out of the pot.

Usually it was a small-stakes game, but one night I was really hitting and I won $80. Everyone else split early, but I stayed and drank and smoked a little marijuana. Smoking grass was a big thing for me, because I felt safe and secure enough to do it. It was still very illegal, although the police pretty much left smokers alone. It was the dealers they arrested, and I never, ever sold even an ounce to anyone else.

As 1973 began I felt more secure than ever before. After nine years and nine months of successfully evading the law, I almost stopped thinking of myself as a fugitive. I was Dennis Simons of San Francisco, a happy, hard-working American citizen. And one afternoon I walked into the local post office and found that, after all these years, the FBI had finally done me a favor.

16

J. Edgar Hoover, director of the Federal Bureau of Investigation, died on May 2, 1972. He had been on my mind so long that in a strange way it was almost like seeing a friend die. I felt older, tired. But I had won. Although officially I was still wanted, and listed number one on the most wanted list, my adventure seemed to end with his death. Hoover, more than the agency, had been my adversary. And I had beaten him.

He was replaced by L. Patrick Gray, and I wasn't sure how this was going to affect either me or the FBI. I kept checking to make sure my poster was still hanging in the post office and I didn't dare think about shaving off my beard. Richard Kimble was now rerunning and Efrem Zimbalist's ratings had really fallen off and it looked like the program wasn't going to run too much longer. I wasn't exactly a free man, but I was freer.

Early in February 1973, I walked into the post office and, as usual, wandered over to the bulletin board. I made a quick check, but I didn't see the poster, so I looked a little more carefully. The harder I looked, the more excited I got. The poster wasn't there!

I kept my emotions in check and went to another area, where they hung dozens of other fugitives who didn't make the list. I looked over every photograph, I read every name. John William Clouser was not there! I was off the list.

I wanted to leap into the air and shout hysterically, but I walked out almost as casually as I had walked in. To my knowledge no one had ever been taken off the list without being killed or captured. Now, for the first time, I really knew without a doubt that I had it made for the rest of my life.

And I had no one to tell. Margy didn't know I was a federal fugitive, a top ten criminal, so it would be difficult to tell her that all of a sudden I wasn't one. Of course, the fact that I wasn't hanging in the post office didn't mean I was no longer a fugitive—it just meant they had given up trying to find me. If I got into trouble, or if someone discovered my past, I could still be in jail for a long time. So I kept quiet, but I was immensely happy inside.

Margy picked it up right away. "What are you so excited about?"

"Oh, nothing," I told her. "Are you making dinner?"

She told me she was. "Pot roast."

"Listen," I said as casually as I could, "after you finish the pot roast, don't you feel it's time you and I got married?"

She let out a happy yell and came running into the living room and threw her arms around me.

"I'm the happiest woman in the world," she laughed.

"I'm the happiest man in the world," I laughed. I was, I really was. She had wanted to get married since her divorce had become final, but I kept putting her off. I had been married in Florida, but June had filed for divorce while I was in the mental institution, and I assumed she followed through with it. So now that I was no longer on the top ten I didn't see any reason to wait any longer.

"When?" she wanted to know.

I was ready to tell her immediately, but I decided that I wanted to take one last fling, a final trip by myself. I wanted to get the last of my playing around out of my system. "As soon as I come back from my trip," we agreed.

This trip, almost a victory celebration, was an ocean voyage to South America. Once again I took my form from the notary public—it would have been impossible for me to ever get a passport—and climbed aboard in Miami, Florida.

Florida. It had been almost exactly nine years since I left, and as my plane landed I instinctively caught myself looking around, watching every face. For a few minutes I was on the run again, hiding. I knew what could happen if I should get caught.

I also knew my sons were somewhere in the state and my heart hurt when I thought about them. God, how desperately I wanted to know about them!

I didn't really relax until the ship left port and sailed for the Bahamas. We toured the Bahamas and then on to Puerto Rico. For meals I was assigned to sit at the flag captain's table. On nights like this I enjoyed a private laugh wondering what the people I was sitting with would do if they knew my secret. Among the other guests at the table were Mike and Jeannie Murphy. Mike Murphy is one of the best private detectives in San Francisco. And we sat and we talked and we became friends, the private detective and the hunted man. He never suspected the slightest thing about me. There was no reason why he should have.

I had three unusual bunkmates that trip. The first was an elderly man dying of a heart attack. The second was another very old man

163

with two broken hips. The third was a homosexual Englishman who got seasick and spent most of the voyage being sick. Needless to say, I didn't spend too much time in the cabin.

We made stops at the Virgin Islands, Antigua, Barbados, and then down into Venezuela. I was spending a good deal of time with Mike Murphy, who was justifiably proud of his work. The more he talked about what he had accomplished, the more I wanted to tap him on the shoulder and ask if he ever heard of Jack Clouser. I had an ego too!

From Venezuela we hit the Dutch Antilles, then Panama, then Acapulco, and eventually San Francisco.

When I walked off that ship my wandering days were over. From that point on, I knew, Margy and I would never be separated. On April 15, ten years and two weeks since my escape, we took a bus to Reno, Nevada, to get married. On the way I thought about that dark night in the Georgia hills. I had asked God for ten years of freedom and he had given them to me. Plus. I felt I lived up to my part of the bargain. I'd led an honest life and earned my way into real society.

Our wedding was beautiful. A black minister conducted the service and told us, "I'm gonna tie you two so tight you ain't never gonna get loose!" Marge cried, she was so happy, and I was too. I felt like all the women I had known and all the sexual experiences I had had were just preparation for this moment. I had the woman I loved and I was marrying her. As far as I was concerned, this was just the first day of the rest of our lives together.

Our life together got better and better after the marriage. Margy kept her promise to cut down her activities and we spent all our free time together. We had tickets to the San Francisco Forty-Niner football games and the San Francisco Opera. We had credit cards from the local gas stations and department stores. I even went so far as to get a California driver's license. I paid a friend of mine $50 to go down to the motor vehicle bureau, register as me, take the driving test, be fingerprinted, and obtain a license in the name of Dennis Ray Simons. Once I had the license I bought another car. I registered it under the name of Dennis Ray Simons, just to confuse the computers. I paid my income tax every year to the federal and state governments. I was playing a lot of golf. We had a lot of friends, and life was just wonderful. We were an ordinary couple doing ordinary things. It was better than I had thought possible.

All I had to do was spend the rest of my life without getting

164

arrested or giving a fingerprint anywhere and we would be happy forever.

Margy started working for the Pacific Telephone Company in early 1974 as a computer operator, and by hard work she became shop steward union representative. I started working at Goss and Goss Putty and Caulking factory, doing a million different little jobs and loving every minute of it. We were both busy with our jobs, and our relationship began to suffer.

Margy started getting wrapped up in union work. It took the place of her other involvement, and once again I started playing the second role in her life. I wanted to go to the movies, she had a meeting. I wanted to go to a show, she had to make recruitment phone calls. Naturally—naturally for me, at least—I got jealous and resentful. I started playing around again.

She was working very hard to make extra money to put her son through college. Since he and I didn't really get along, I didn't feel it was my place to help him. It was these little things that built into the worst situation of my running life.

On the night of June 8, 1974, it all ended, with one tragic, unbelievable incident. Margy was working sixteen hours that day, so, just to keep from being bored, I went to the wrestling matches and afterward stopped in at the local bar for a quick drink. Len Uhlman was there with Dianne Hamilton and I could see right away that both of them were pretty wiped out. Another friend of ours, Johnny Witte, was there too. So I sat down with my friends Lenny and Johnny and Dianne and we ordered one drink, then another, and another. We were talking about all the times we'd spent together, all the laughs, all the happy days. Finally Dianne asked Johnny and I to do her a favor. There was a guy crashing on her couch and would we get him out of her apartment? Sure, we told her, sure, eventually.

In the meantime we proceeded to get very happily drunk. Dianne and I staggered to my car and somewhere along the way Johnny disappeared. I didn't really care, this sounded like an easy job for me to handle. We drove to her apartment.

I never, ever should have gone there. It was one of the worst mistakes I ever made in my life. This woman was crazy. I had been warned. But I just wouldn't listen.

At first everything was fine. The stranger was sleeping on her couch. I shook him and he half woke up, at least he opened his eyes. It was obvious he was up on some sort of drugs and was really only semiconscious. I picked him up by his belt and not so gently walked him downstairs, threatening to throw him out if he ever came back.

I watched him slowly fade down the street, then I walked back upstairs. Dianne was really impressed with the way I'd handled the situation. But I wasn't going to stay with her or make love to her. I really, truly wasn't.

"It's late," I explained. "My wife is in bed and I'm going to take off now. Don't worry, he won't be back."

"No, wait. Let's smoke one joint. Just one."

We smoked one joint.

"I've got to go now," I said, not quite so convincingly as the first time.

"No, not yet. Let's smoke one more joint." She got up and put out all the lights. Then she lit candles all over the room, creating a very warm, romantic atmosphere.

We smoked another joint. I was really loosening up.

"Things are really getting better," she was saying. "I'm doing real good at the psychiatrist's now and he says—"

I think she wants me to make love to her, I thought.

"—and so when I went to see him he said that—"

I'm going to lean over and start right now.

"—healthy and so very soon too. I told him that I wanted to—"

I leaned over and gave her a nice, big kiss. She felt very warm against me and didn't resist at all. I pulled her closer, and I could feel her breathing start to get heavier. Her hips were pushing against mine, and her mouth just melted right into mine. In the middle of the kiss, without breaking the mood, I picked her up and carried her into the bedroom and laid her down on the bed. I slid down beside her and we both stretched our bodies into each other. Her arms went around my back and her hands were running up and down my whole upper body. I dug my kiss deeper into her. We were upping the passion, moving quickly. I started to unbutton her blouse.

She reached up to my head and yanked my hair back hard, pulling my mouth right off hers.

I grabbed a handful of her hair and pulled right back. It seemed like a silly game.

"Hey, honey," I told her, "you're getting a little rough, aren't you?"

166

She screamed. "You bastard! I hate you! I can't make love!" And she grabbed my right arm and pinched it very hard.

I stopped completely. I had been through this sort of freak-out scene before and I didn't want to go through it again.

"Hey, Dianne, that wasn't necessary. All you have to do is tell me no. You didn't have to hurt me, you know."

She was almost in a trance. She was looking at me and talking, but she wasn't speaking to *me*. "It's horrible. I'm afraid you won't believe this, but I've been having these terrible nightmares. . . ." Now she realized I was there, listening to her. "It's horrible, I don't know what to do. I'm just freaking out."

All I wanted to do was keep her calm and get out of there quickly.

"Dianne, you know I like you. You know I'm your friend, right? You've really got a problem and you've had it since I met you. I'm going home to my wife now, where I should have gone an hour ago, and I'll see you later. O.K.?"

"O.K.," she agreed.

I thought everything was finished and fine. I spent the next day cutting the grass, watering our flowers, and watching a golf match on television. Margy cooked dinner, we had a few drinks sitting on the bed and were watching TV.

There was a loud banging on the door. I knew instinctively it was the end of the world.

I opened the door to see three members of the San Francisco police department. My heart fell. "Are you Dennis Simons?"

"Yes." I didn't know what it was about, but I knew it wasn't good.

"We have a warrant for your arrest. Can we come in and talk about it?"

Be calm, I kept warning myself, be cool. I tried to remember my story, but I quickly realized I didn't need a story. I *was* Dennis Simons. "Certainly, come on in."

They walked into the living room. In my mind I was trying to put together as many facts as possible. But my mind wasn't working perfectly. I had become confident and soft over the past few years and I had almost forgotten those lessons I had learned so hard. My mind was quickly trying to restructure the proper thought chain. I had to think at least one step ahead of the police if I had the slightest chance of surviving.

A sergeant did the talking for the cops. "May I look at your arm?"

The pinch mark, Dianne Hamilton, that's what it was all about. For a brief instant I figured I might have some hope. I held out my arm and rolled up my sleeve. The mark was there, bright and black and blue.

"Where'd you get that pinch mark?"

They evidently had one side of the story. I couldn't make up an obvious lie. I had to work with them, gain their confidence, use the truth, at least at first. "I got it fooling around with my girl friend last night. She pinched me."

The sergeant almost looked embarrassed, as if he knew exactly what had happened. I had had calls like that in Orlando. A girl friend got sore at her boy friend and called the police and charged him. The charges were invariably dropped.

The sergeant took a deep breath. "Mr. Simons, you must be kidding me. You've been charged with assault to rape."

I just stood there with my mouth opened. These policemen had no idea that they were arresting one of the most successful fugitives in America. All they had was a simple assault charge. But it was enough, more than enough. It was the end.

"You'll have to come with us."

I muttered something like, "O.K." Slowly, like a tired machine, my mind started creaking into use. I knew what my assets were: identification, money and another identification safely hidden in the house, and time. If I could get away from them before they could get my fingerprints checked in Washington, I could still make my getaway.

Getaway? Leave Margy?

I had no choice. My life in San Francisco was finished.

Margy had stayed in the bedroom all this time. Now she finally wandered into the living room and asked me what the trouble was. I had to look her right in the eye and be totally honest with her. "Margy, I didn't come straight home from the wrestling matches last night. I was fooling around with Dianne Hamilton. She freaked out and charged me with assault." I died inside as I told her that, but I really had no choice.

She just stared at me and didn't say anything. But as long as I live I'll never forget the look of pain in her eyes. She wasn't upset that I had lied to her, but the fact that I was being arrested and taken away hurt her a lot.

"We're going to take him to the Mission Avenue Station," the

168

sergeant told Margy, "and then around midnight he'll be transferred to the Hall of Justice. You can bond him out then if you can find a bondsman that will write a bond for him. Do you understand?"

She said she did, and she repeated the information to him.

"Can I say good-bye to my wife?" I asked. They nodded. I put my arms around her very tightly. We were both doing our best to hold back the tears.

"I love you so very much," I said, "and I need your help. I guess this is the end of everything. Take the money I have here and the identification I have with it and try to get me out. Please, try to get me out." I told her once again that I loved her, and walked out with the cops.

The moment we walked out the door, Dennis Ray Simons died and John William Clouser was reborn.

Jack Clouser. On the ride downtown I rolled the name over my tongue a few times. It sounded strange. I had ceased being him so many lifetimes ago, so many adventures ago. And now it was all coming home. I had to run if I got the opportunity.

If I got the opportunity.

17

"You are under arrest, charged with assault to rape. You have the right to remain silent. You have the right to an attorney. An attorney may be present whenever you are questioned. . . ."

I listened to my rights being read, but I really didn't pay too much attention. My mind was snapping back quickly now, and I was looking for any advantage.

"Now," the sergeant asked me, "would you like to tell us what happened last night?"

I gave a somewhat phony laugh. "It's a bum rap. I met her in a bar, she's a friend of a good friend of mine, and she asked me to go home with her and throw out some guy sleeping on her couch. I did, we had a few drinks and started fooling around." I lifted my head up and looked the sergeant right in the face. "Then she freaked out. When you check you'll find she's got a history of mental illness. I never touched her, I swear I never touched her. The charges are going to be dropped tomorrow, there's no question about that." I paused. "Look, how often do you get girl friends accusing their boy friends of rape because they're mad at them?"

"It happens," the sergeant agreed.

"That's exactly what happened this time. I swear to God." I was really pleading with him. I was willing to do anything to avoid being fingerprinted. "Is there any way possible they could keep from booking me until I've spoken to her? It would mean an awful lot to me."

I think he would have liked to avoid the paper work, but the law is the law is the law. "I can't. Sorry, but it's against the law to even talk to somebody who's made a complaint against you."

Sunday night, June 9, at nine o'clock, I was put in a holding cell. I knew I still had a slim chance. If Margy could bail me out and get downtown with my money and identification before the San Francisco police had a chance to check my fingerprints with the FBI computers in Washington, D.C., I could make a run for it.

With luck I was going out on the road again. I didn't want to run. I was tired. I was happy. I wanted my job at the putty factory and my cottage and my season tickets to the opera and the football games, and most of all, Margy. Each second in that cell was agony. Any minute I expected the FBI to walk into the station and arrest me as a federal fugitive named John William Clouser.

At midnight I was moved downtown to the Hall of Justice, along

170

with the regular weekend crowd of drunks and fighters and knifers. They gave me a quick skin search—naturally I was clean—and took all my property and put me in another hold tank.

I paced the floor for an hour. Waiting, just waiting. I wanted my freedom so badly I could feel it in every pore. But instead I faced return to a mental institution in Florida. The whole nightmare was going to start again.

About twelve-thirty one of the jailers came to the cell and said, "Simons, your wife just made bail for you. She's downstairs waiting."

Maybe, just maybe, I was going to beat this one too.

"Well, when can I go?"

"Soon. We just got to book you and process you first, then we'll let you go. Not too long."

How long is a life of freedom? Not too long? I disagreed with the jailer. A little while later a Mexican officer came in and took out one of the drunks. He processed him, too slowly. C'mon, c'mon, I silently pleaded.

The Mexican policeman came back to the cell. "Simons," he called out.

I got up quickly. "Here." I knew I had to be supercool. If he became the least bit suspicious it would destroy my slim lifeline of hope. Right away I decided to lay a story on him. "Boy, you don't know how embarrassing this is. I gotta go downstairs and explain to my wife what I was doing last night with my girl friend."

"We get these all the time, she'll understand. O.K., now give me your right hand." He took my fingerprints from me. I watched as each little spot of ink was stamped onto the white cards. Tiny spots, none more than an inch, but each of them marking the end of a wonderful life. He took four, five, six, seven sets of my fingerprints. Even if I managed to get out of the hall before Washington got my prints, once they matched them the hunt would be on again.

He put two sets in a pneumatic cylinder and they whooshed upstairs. I knew they would go to the state of California computers first. I had nothing to worry about, I was clean in California. Then they would go to the FBI computer center in Washington. The countdown had begun.

Finally, wonderfully, he told me I could go and I started to take off. I was ready to run downstairs and grab Margy—but he shouted and stopped me dead in my tracks.

"Jesus," he laughed, "I almost forgot to take your picture."

We went into the mug room and he started snapping away. New pictures for my wanted posters, I thought. Then the ringing of the telephone smashed the silence. He answered and listened for a moment. Then he stared at me. He spoke into the phone. "Are you serious?" Then he paused. "He's finished and he's ready to go. I can't hold him, you know what the laws are. He's bonded. I got to let him go." He paused again. "Well, you'd better hurry."

I didn't have to be told what the subject of their conversation was. I laughed inside. I was so close to making it. Another sixty seconds and I would have been out. Free. Running again. But I was caught and all because I didn't know enough to stay away from a mentally sick woman.

He was still talking on the telephone. "What'd you do last weekend? You see Billy?" I knew he was stalling for time until the FBI agents arrived.

Finally he hung up and looked at me. "Well, now, Dennis, I'm afraid I'm going to have to put you back in a holding cell for fifteen minutes."

I *had* to get out of that station. I boiled up my almost forgotten temper and got goddam indignant.

"Now you look," I bluffed. "I'm bonded out and you have to let me go. I heard you say that yourself. My wife is downstairs and I'm leaving!"

"Don't get so excited, relax," he told me, "it's only some traffic problem. I promise, only fifteen minutes." I had no choice but to return to the holding cell. I didn't know what to do. I paced.

He went right to the desk sergeant with the photographs, and I knew that was the very end. I'd never get out. They both examined them, occasionally looking over toward me. I said nothing.

Fifteen minutes later, true to his word, he took me out of the cell. "Go see the desk sergeant."

Now all I had to do was get my belongings and I was gone. I knew the difference between freedom and bars was going to be a few minutes.

The sergeant stalled. He took three minutes to walk from the water fountain to his desk. "O.K.," he said, "sign this property slip." He started rummaging through the papers on his desk, but he couldn't find the slip. He kept pulling out file after file, and I knew that any second the FBI was going to come walking through the big front door.

172

All of a sudden he started screaming at one of the officers, "You dummy, you put the wrong number on here." He pushed it toward me. "Sign it."

I did. Then he couldn't find my belongings. I was even more positive that, at any second, the door was going to fly open and the FBI, led by Efrem Zimbalist, would come streaking into the room to destroy my life.

The door opened. But it wasn't the FBI, it was simply another San Francisco policeman, carrying my personal belongings. They had been misplaced, I was told. I grabbed them and walked out the door to the elevator.

I was no longer in a hurry. I knew for sure that the lobby just had to be full of FBI agents. Ten years of trustworthy vibrations told me it was absolutely true. Paranoia? No way. They were there.

Slowly I climbed onto the elevator and pressed the lobby button. The elevator started descending. My stomach was churning. I reached the lobby with a slight bump and the doors split open. It was a scene I will never forget.

The room was completely deserted except for Margy. She sat alone, on a bench, her head in her hands, her tears falling onto her dress. I grabbed her and held her and gave her a big kiss.

"You're wonderful," I said happily, "and I love you so very much. Now let's get out of here."

I drove away from the Hall of Justice like a madman. I knew I had four hours at best to get out of San Francisco, four hours before the FBI opened in Washington and my prints were checked.

The Florida Fox was on the run again.

I threw a few things into a small traveling bag and got out of the cottage in five minutes. Margy drove me to the parking lot of an all-night hamburger place and we parked there to wait for daylight and the first bus out of town. We just sat in the car and held each other and cried. I told her over and over how sorry I was, how stupid I was, and how desperately I loved her.

"I don't care what you did," she said through her tears. "What's going to happen to you?" Our hearts were just breaking.

"I don't know. I don't know. I'll just have to see." Margy still didn't know my real name or anything that I had been accused of in the past. All she knew was that I had been in trouble in the past and those troubles had caught up to me and I had to flee. I didn't tell her more than that because I didn't want to make her guilty of harboring a fugitive.

At seven-thirty I put my arms around her as hard as I could, kissed her tenderly, and said, "I love you and I'll come back to you," and climbed out of the car. I took one deep breath and looked around for police cars. Nothing was happening in the area. I was alone again, running again, and very lonely.

The very first thing I did was go into the men's room and shave off the beard I'd worn for the last three years. I looked in the mirror and I didn't even recognize the face that peered back at me. I hadn't seen that face in years, and it had only changed slightly. I got a terrible chill as I looked at that stranger's eyes.

I walked into the bus station and bought a ticket for Oakland. I wasn't particularly nervous yet because I knew the prints couldn't have been identified so quickly. There was about a twenty-minute wait before my bus left, and I just had to call Lenny Uhlman. I had to straighten him out.

It was difficult to believe Dianne called the cops without his knowledge. After I'd gotten him a job and all, I didn't understand why he would let her do it. He *knew* she was crazy. He knew me well enough to know I would never try to rape anyone. I was totally and completely nonviolent, I didn't believe in hurting people except in self-defense. And I had all the sex I wanted just by asking.

I woke him up. "Lenny, about last night," I started, trying to keep my temper. "Why didn't you call me and ask me what happened? I thought you were supposed to be my friend."

He was really apologetic. "I'm sorry, Dennis, we're going to go right down to the station this morning and drop the charges. We got pretty high and, you know, it was a mistake."

"Why didn't you just call me? Why didn't you do that?"

"Oh, I don't know. We didn't think about it."

"Don't you realize I would never hurt Dianne? Don't you realize she's fantasizing, that she imagined herself being ravished? Don't you know those things, Len, as long as we've been friends?" I think he probably heard the desperation in my voice.

"Yeah, I know it now. But we just weren't thinking very clearly yesterday. You got to understand that. I promise you, we're going to get the charges dropped first thing this morning. It was all a big mistake."

174

I almost laughed at the irony. "It's too late, Lenny, it's just too late."

He started waking up. "What do you mean?"

"Len, I'm gonna tell you something. My name is not Dennis Ray Simons. I'm a federal fugitive and I've been on the top ten most wanted list for years. I've got to run for my life now. You and Dianne did something the whole FBI couldn't do, you smoked me out. What do I care about this little piddly charge? You smoked me out and now I have to give up everything." As I spoke to him the realization of what I was saying started to overcome the shock I had been in. "Everything. My wife, my home, my job, Marge'll lose our money in the bank because I have to jump bond. Everything!"

"Oh, my God!" he said softly, and I knew he really was sorry for what he had done. "Is that the truth? I can't believe it." He didn't wait for an answer, he just kept talking. "What can we do to help, Dennis? Tell me what to do. Anything."

I held my breath for a second and cleared my eyes. "The only chance I've got, the only thing I can ask you to do, is you and Dianne go down and get those charges dropped so Margy won't lose our savings and she'll have something to live on."

"I give you my word, Dennis, we'll do that. We'll save the bond money for your wife. I promise."

The bus was getting ready to leave so I had to hang up. "So long, Lenny. Say good-bye to all the guys for me. Maybe I'll see you again someday."

He didn't know what to say. "Dennis, I'm really sorry. We just didn't know."

"Nobody did," I said almost jokingly, "before."

From Oakland I went to Reno and checked into the St. Francis Hotel. My plan was to get as far away from San Francisco as quickly as I could. I thought I might go to Canada first and try to size up the situation. I'd met some people on the South American cruise who lived there, and I knew they would put me up.

After a night in Reno I got up very early, got my hair cut short, and went out to the airport to catch a plane to Minneapolis, Minnesota. At the airport I went into the paperback bookstore to get something to read to keep my mind occupied. After the initial shock of my arrest and narrow escape had worn off, something else almost overwhelmed me. Pure terror. For years I had been reading and studying the exploits of the FBI, and just too often cases ended with someone being shot dead. After making fools of the agency for a full decade I was petrified about what they would do if they caught me. They could easily take me out and shoot me down and justify their actions by saying I had originally escaped from a mental institution and had tried to escape from them. I needed something to read to forget about the agency.

One book with a dark-blue cover more or less leaped at me. It was called *Killer*, and it was written by an organized crime hit man, Joey, with a writer named Dave Fisher. I bought the book and started reading it. The long introduction told about how Joey and Fisher met, and described the relationship the two of them had. They became friends, and the result was the book. I reread the introduction. And reread it again. Then I started reading the book itself.

We made stopovers in Salt Lake City and in Denver. I just sat quietly in my seat, watching everybody on the plane, reading my book. By now my fingerprints must have drawn some attention in both Washington, D.C., and San Francisco. I felt somewhat safe on the plane, but I knew it was only a temporary feeling. I had to get used to living with fear all over again.

When we finally got to Minneapolis I checked into a cheap hotel and immediately dyed my hair from blond to brown. Now, with my beard gone, my hair short, and its color changed, I looked nothing like the man in the mug shots taken two nights before. My plan was to sit in the hotel for two full days, take a bus across the border to Winnipeg, then go to Vancouver, get a Canadian passport, and go to Australia to start another brand-new life.

I laid in that hotel room thinking about being on the run again. It was so difficult to believe that I had to give up everything again, my friends, my wife, my life. I cried myself to sleep both nights just longing for Marge. I knew I could run again, and again, and maybe establish another life, but still have to go through the whole thing again and again. I knew I would never really be safe until I faced those terrible charges waiting for me in Orlando, Florida. I actually began to think about surrendering. Giving up, after all these years.

My thoughts drifted from place to place during those forty-eight hours. I kept reading *Killer*, but I would continually go back to the introduction.

And then I would think of going back to prison. Prison! When I thought about that I knew I couldn't surrender. Even life as a fugitive was better than the so-called life behind bars.

176

But I couldn't abandon Margy. I had never really been in love before; I had never met a woman like her before.

I had to surrender.

I had to keep running.

Over and over I considered the possibilities. The last years of my life had been spent just like any other good citizen. Every thought in my head, every molecule in my body had changed. I had studied philosophy, there was no malice or hatred left in me. I was a member of the Fraternal Order of Eagles, a benevolent association that helps handicapped children. My wife had taught me about the arts, and we'd spent days in art galleries, and I even started painting myself. We had friends, we'd go to barbecues, parties, exchange gifts. I had worked hard and had a good record at American Can and now at the putty factory. All of that had to prove something, didn't it?

I just couldn't be sure. I had been involved in some terrible things in Orlando and I knew the people I left behind there hadn't changed as I had. My supposed crimes were still on the books and I knew I would have to stand trial for them. I also knew there was absolutely no way I could get a fair trial in Orlando, Florida.

Run again, and again?

Surrender and go back behind bars?

I put off making a decision. In Winnipeg, I figured, I would have time to really make the right choice.

The third day I pulled my few belongings together and bought myself a bus ticket for Canada. I waited at the door for the bus to appear, my mind just overrun with the thoughts of the last few days. The long silver bus pulled in on time and started loading up. I stood there as the other passengers walked past me and climbed aboard. I just stood watching and waiting, for what I wasn't sure. But I didn't move. I couldn't get on that bus. I stood motionless as it pulled out of its dock and started its trip north.

The time had finally come.

Ten long years ago in the Georgia dirt I promised God if he would give me ten years of freedom I would lead an honest life. I would never steal as long as he would show me the way. He showed me the way. The ten years ended on the most ridiculous stroke of fate and the same situation couldn't happen again in a hundred years. But I'm convinced that, if it hadn't happened, some other thing would've brought the ten years to an end.

The best thing I could do to prove my sincerity in wanting to live an honest, decent life was to offer my body to the establishment, with the hope and faith that someday I would be free again to resume the life I loved with my wife and my little cottage and my friends in San Francisco.

So instead of going to Winnipeg, I caught the next bus to Chicago. I had only a few more miles left to travel. And only a few more months of freedom.

18

Dear Mr. Fisher:

I am writing to you as an intramediary for a third party. He has one of the most fantastic, unbelievable, thrilling, heartbreaking stories that has ever happened in America.

He is an infamous person. If I told you his name you'd probably know it. His story is about the last twelve years mostly, and ten years of that involves a branch of the federal government. It has been more or less suppressed and kept very low key, and has been a source of embarrassment to the government. It's time for this story to be told. . . .

My letter to Dave Fisher in New York went on for seven pages. I signed it John Curry and gave the flophouse I was staying in as a return address. I paced the floor for five days, waiting for his return letter. When it came it said he was interested in knowing more about the story, and suggested I write or phone. There was no reason for me to stay where I was. I took the next bus to New York City to meet Joey's collaborator.

I stayed in New York, taping my story, for more than two months, while we negotiated with a publisher and worked on my surrender plans. In that time I started making phone calls and slowly managed to reconstruct my life. From a story about me in a detective magazine I learned that my mother had died in 1970 and my first wife had committed suicide.

I phoned my father. "It's Jack," I said to him. "It's your son."

There was a long silence on the other end of the phone. "My son is dead," he finally said.

"Come on, Dad, don't be silly. It's me, it's Jack."

He kept protesting, "I have no son."

"Don't you remember? The last time we saw each other was in an alley. You put your arms around me and told me you loved me."

He didn't answer. He couldn't.

My sister got on the telephone and we went through the whole process again. "Is it really you?"

"It's really me."

"No, it's not."

"Yes, it is. Remember the day the detectives arrested me and you had an epileptic fit?" I finally convinced her and she began to tell me all about my family. She told me the little she knew about my sons in Orlando.

My sons! The thought of seeing them again was both frightening and exciting. I was afraid June ruined my boys, I was scared they would be like her. But I had to see them, I was desperate.

I was still being very, very careful about preserving my freedom. Now that I had decided to surrender I wanted to walk in on my own, I didn't want to be dragged in before I was ready. I obtained a lawyer, James Siff of New York City. He made arrangements with doctors at Mt. Sinai Hospital to examine me and determine my mental state. Both Siff and I were worried that Orlando officials might try to stick me back in Chattahoochee and forget about me. The doctors and examinations proved I was perfectly sane.

One afternoon in Siff's office I made the most difficult telephone call of my life. "June," I started, "this is Jack. How you been?"

June was just as feisty as ever, but it sounded good to hear her voice. We talked about a dozen different things, but mostly about the boys. She told me they were fine, and happy and good kids. Then she put Tony on the phone.

"Tony, this is your father." The five most wonderful words I had ever spoken. From their voices they both sounded like June had raised them well.

Things kept happening so fast I had a difficult time keeping track of events. Margy told me in one of our secret phone calls—I had her be in a particular phone booth at a certain time—that the San Francisco police had been to see her a number of times. She also told me there was someone constantly sitting in a parked car on the corner—the police, I assumed.

Time just whizzed by. Siff made arrangements with officials in Orlando for me to surrender. As the day came closer and closer I steeled myself for the inevitable. I knew what I was going back to. But I also knew what was waiting for me if I successfully managed to regain my freedom.

Fisher, Siff, a photographer named David Burnett, and myself all flew down to Tallahassee in early August. Paul Cunningham, reporter at large for the "Today" show, was at the airport with a film crew. My surrender had been arranged. I knew cameramen and reporters would be waiting for me.

As we drove into the state capital for my surrender, I considered what I had been through the whole last decade. I had learned the greatest lesson of all. There is only one thing that really matters in life—to love someone and have them love you equally in return. I had found Margy. Through her all the hostility, revenge, and aggression I ever had in my soul and mind had disappeared. Through her I found contentment, peace of mind, happiness, tranquillity, everything that's important to be able to live a happy life.

The car stopped a few blocks from the criminal building and we all piled out. I walked straight ahead, keeping my head high.

Ten years. Finished, now. My life was starting all over again. Ten years on the run from the finest policemen in the world. Why had I been so successful? I thought about it with each step. I had managed to disguise my appearance with hats and glasses and hair colors and lengths—both growing it and shaving it off. I had always done my best to present a good appearance and not to draw attention to myself. I'd worked hard and decided right at the beginning that I was going to be honest. And I was, I was.

I thought about the discipline I had managed to maintain, the times I wanted to lose my temper and held myself back. The nights I cried myself to sleep thinking about my sons and desperately wanting to contact them and hear their voices, but knowing I couldn't. The terrible frustration of knowing the fact that I was innocent didn't matter to society. I was the escapee, I was the psychopath, I was the cop gone bad.

I thought about the little mental tricks I had taught myself to remember who I was supposed to be and where I was supposed to be from and what I was supposed to be doing and all the other bits and pieces of information that make up a life.

There are two kinds of fugitives. One, the moment he gets his freedom, all he wants to do is pick up his gun and get revenge and live through crime. Very few of this type survive. The other type are the people who are so grateful and happy to be free that they'll do anything to blend into the society they live in, and cherish each day of freedom. I learned to cherish each and every day. I learned what freedom really means.

I turned the corner. My life as the most wanted man in America was over.

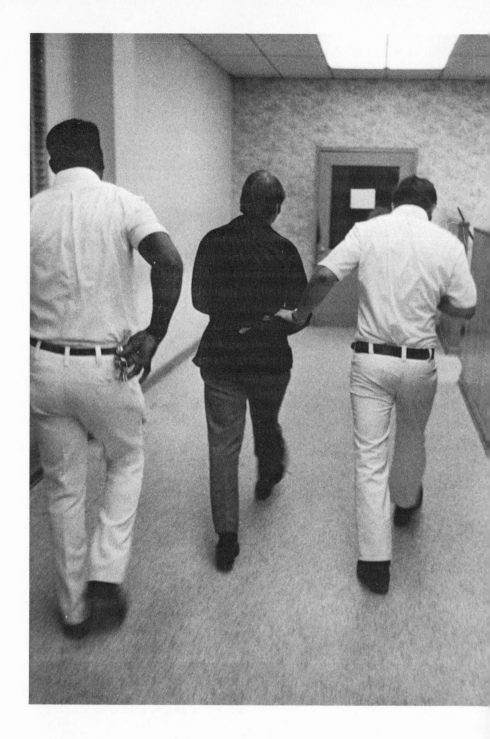

After his surrender in August 1974, Clouser was led away in handcuffs. *Photo*: David Burnett, Gamma.

EPILOGUE

Friday, August 23, 1974
Florida State Hospital at Chattahoochee
DEAR DAVE,

All I've done here for the first two days is sign autographs. I am on no medication except for "Esidrex." They say it's for a salt free diet. Mail is uncensored both ways. I have done no psychological testing yet, only written a three page letter about myself to the doctor. I don't think they are in any hurry to send me down to Orlando. It's just dead time here, waiting to be tested.

Things are good here. I played basketball and badmitton both this morning and feel good. Not like New York when I just had to lay around in hiding. Write soon, regards to all who knew me in New York. You can tell them my real name now.

Your friend,
Jack

Tuesday, August 27, 1974

DEAR DAVE,

June has made statements charging me with bigamy. It seems she never went through with the divorce. I usually have enough trouble staying married to one woman. Now I've got two!

June keeps saying I deserted her and my boys. She seems to have forgotten the fact that she testified against me, like that had nothing to do with it.

It's really strange being back in Florida after all these years. The institutions have changed; the people haven't.

I have had no tests yet and I am getting anxious. I haven't seen my sons yet. I wonder if June has turned them against me.

Sincerely,
Jack

P.S. I just spoke to Jimmy Siff. Allie Brown believes that I implicated his brother Jackie in the liquor store holdup, when I never did any such thing. Jackie spent a lot of time in jail and died just after he got out, so Allie is blaming it all on me. I really don't remember at all the liquor store robbery. I escaped shortly thereafter and never saw Allie or Jackie again.

183

Wednesday, August 28, 1974

DEAR DAVE,

A newspaper reporter came today with June and the boys. Wow, what boys! They're mine, they're my sons! I think they love me. What a wonderful feeling it was to see them. At first they held back, but by the end of their visit we were really getting along. I am wild about my boys. Timmy has a need, a real need for me. He hugged me so tight and told me that he loved me when he left. Tony is too tough for that kind of need, but not Timmy. And I am so happy.

I took my first test today.

Margy has twelve of our friends willing to co-sign any bail papers for me, and a close friend in San Francisco, John Garcia, has three or four more. I heard that Eagan, the district attorney on the case, has said, off the record, that he has no case, that he couldn't prosecute me. I don't believe it. They're just sandbagging, hoping to catch us off guard. They're working on at least one charge, I'm positive.

Your friend,
Jack

Monday, September 9, 1974

DEAR DAVE,

First, I never signed any papers or statements about Jackie Brown being involved in the liquor store robbery. But for some reason, Allie is still convinced that I implicated his brother. I only said, "Not guilty, I don't know anything about it."

I enjoyed the story in the *New York Post*, except for one thing. Don't say I was a crooked cop. I was once an honest, dedicated cop, eventually corrupted by the system.

I am going to set up a trust fund for all my children with any money I get from our book. I do love my sons and I intend to give them everything.

The papers are still printing stories all the time. Prosecutor Robert Eagan made some strong statements about my case. He's beginning to worry me. . . . There's no statute of limitations on crimes a man has been indicted for. Once you're indicted the charges never expire. . . . I'm not sure how many potential witnesses are still alive. I'm not worried about that, if they're honest they can't hurt me.

Life here at Chattahoochee is still O.K. They are really professional people here, things have really changed. They no longer keep the inmates drugged all the time, the wards are integrated, the staff is

184

helpful and friendly. Make sure we say some nice things about this place, they're deserved.

Your friend,
Jack

Friday, September 13, 1974

DEAR DAVE,

At last I got a staff date for my mental examination, Tuesday September 24th, 34 days after my surrender.

I got my first letter ever from my sons. It was from Tony and I would like to quote one paragraph to you from the letter. "A lot of people have been asking me if I've seen you on television. I say I sure have and I'm proud of you because you are my Dad, and I love you." I was so overwhelmed I couldn't hold back the tears. It really got to me. I sent it to Margy for safekeeping because every time I read it I get choked up. Then a new emotion sweeps me, blind panic. What if Eagan robs me of my chance to be a father and love my sons? I don't think I can survive it again.

Everyone's name should be changed in the book. When I escaped from Chattahoochee Marshall and Allie Brown had both been convicted of armed robbery and sentenced to thirty years. I did not know until I surrendered that both convictions were overthrown and they were convicted of conspiracy and given time served.

Your friend,
Jack

Tuesday, September 17, 1974

DEAR DAVE,

I must tell you this story. I've gotten very friendly with the aides here; they're terrific people. One of them told me some of the kids in his neighborhood were playing and he heard them shout, "Let's play Fugitive. O.K., you be the Florida Fox and I'll be the FBI. Bang, I caught you."

"Oh, no, you can't catch me, I'm the Florida Fox!" I laughed all day after I heard this.

I know a lot of my story on the tapes sounds like I was having fun, but I suffered incredibly during the ten years, four months, and nineteen days on the run. I didn't overelaborate because I didn't want to appear soft or emotional. I believe my loneliness was the reason I was so promiscuous. I was looking for Margy. She is all I ever wanted, and when she would ignore me I reacted in the only way I knew, picking up girls. I want to show the love affair between Margy and myself that *will* last forever. We really do love each other even if I am an immoral bounder at times.

Margy called Sunday. She was tricked into writing a statement about me, by the Orlando Police Department. A San Francisco detective asked her to give a statement about me. She explained how much she loved me and how good our life together had been. The Orlando police took that letter and showed it to June, trying to convince her to testify against me. She doesn't want to take the stand, she knows it's best for the boys.

Your friend,
Jack

Wednesday, September 25, 1974

DEAR DAVE,

I was certified sane after passing all the tests easily yesterday. The doctors are writing a favorable report to Orange County, the Judge, Eagan, and Jimmy Siff. As for Eagan, it is now time to worry about him. He said he will "have a go" at me, meaning he wants to try me.

The report issued here will say I'm not a maximum security risk, not psychotic in any way, and that they would recommend five years probation instead of prosecution. I have the highest regard and respect for the people here, as I was well treated.

I'll be going back to the Orlando County Jail soon and I'm trying to prepare myself mentally. I desperately need to get bond and get out between now and my trial. I know I'll win the trial, I'm looking forward to being cleared in a court of law, as long as it's not in Orlando. There's absolutely no way I can get a fair trial in Orlando.

I'm depressed today, even though the testing went perfect, it hasn't made me feel better at all. I've been thinking back to a poem I wrote when I was in maximum security, and it seems more appropriate than ever.

CONCRETE AND STEEL

My floor is concrete,
My roof is steel,
It's living hell,
How it makes you feel.

186

All around the sides is steel,
And the front is steel bars,
You can't see any people,
Or hear any cars.

Your toilet is concrete,
And your bunk is steel too,
And here comes the roaches,
On the way through.

By morning or by night,
It's the same old sight,
Steel and concrete,
Concrete and steel,
When will it end?

Your friend,
Jack

October 4, 1974

DEAR DAVE,

I should be out of here by now. I passed all those tests 11 days ago.

You're right about me being depressed, I am, extremely. I miss Margy so very much and I wish I could just hold her close. I keep having the same nightmare. Eagan is taking Tony and Timmy away from me and June is standing there and laughing.

It's funny, since I've been here I've had no desire for a drink or sex. My mind has totally eliminated both of them. But worrying about Eagan's power and his vow to destroy me is getting to me. Why are people so vicious and savage? All I want is to resume my place in society and be a father to my sons. It doesn't seem fair. Eagan doesn't know me or anything about me. I'm just a name to further his career. Maybe I'm too preoccupied with him, but I sense another kangaroo trial and I am worried.

Your friend,
Jack

DEAR DAVE,

The jail conditions here have really improved since 1963. Now we can watch television, make a phone call, have a shower, and the food is edible. However, I am more convinced than ever that I will never get a fair trial in central Florida. The Judge, as you know, refused to allow Jimmy Siff to appear in court. He said he could sit at the table, but could not speak in my behalf. Imagine, denying me council of my choice and *no bond* on charges 13 years old, after surrendering, living an honest life for 10½ years, and being a different person.

By now you have spoken with Ed Kirkland, who will represent me in place of Jimmy. He is the best around and is knowledgeable about the case—he represented Marshall in his second trial.

The two FBI men I escaped from in Los Angeles were given one month suspensions, I was told. I haven't seen my boys here yet, now that we're so close hopefully I can see them often, but arrangements are being made for a special visit.

I'm just sick about losing Jimmy. Kirkland says it's not really legal, but they've done illegal things to me for 13 years. Will this nightmare ever end for me?

Sincerely,
Jack

November 8, 1974

DEAR DAVE,

Ed Kirkland has been to West Palm Beach to appeal for bond and they turned him down. Unbelievable! It is illegal for them not to give me bond. The law clearly states that bond can only be denied in a capital crime, and the prosecutor has to show he has ample evidence to at least go to trial. This is not a capital crime and Eagan has shown absolutely nothing.

Before my other Florida attorney, Mr. Cullom, withdrew from the case for Ed Kirkland, he had June come into his office and give depositions. She completely exonerated me in her statements, so there's nothing to worry about in our relationship. She really wants me out for the sake of the boys. Sometimes she can be wonderful.

I'm wasting away physically here with nothing to do.

Tony was to escort the school prom queen to midfield at halftime of the football game, but he didn't have a dinner jacket. So it made me very happy to buy him one so he could be with his sweetheart. Tony is very much in love with his girlfriend and doesn't want to leave Florida. I don't intend to try to make either of them move to California. Both boys love their mother and are devoted to her; so be it. All this suffering I'm doing is worth it just to know they are happy, well-adjusted boys, and I'm happy to experience the thrill of knowing them.

Your friend,
Jack

November 13, 1974

DEAR DAVE,

June came up and visited three hours with me. We talked about everything. She told me that Eagan told her, "I don't know how we are going to convict Jack. I wish he hadn't come back. However, the public demands that I try and convict him."

Talk about sick people. One guy here got six months for failing to return a library book. The Judge is not going to give me a change of venue. I can't get a fair trial here. Just mentioning my name in front of a jury is two strikes against me. I won't get any kind of justice here, it's going to be another railroad job.

Your friend,
Jack

November 22, 1974
San Francisco, California

DEAR DAVE,

Well, the trial is almost here. I try to be confident and I'm thankful that you and Jimmy and Mr. Kirkland are confident. But I can't help feeling the same things Jack worries about in Orlando. I fear they are real meat-grinder courts, "the heart of conservatism, punishment and revenge," in Jack's words. I know he is suffering and believes he will be convicted regardless of whether there are witnesses or not.

Jack has asked that the Eagle Club and I write letters to the judge and we have done this, he said it probably wouldn't do any good, but it wouldn't hurt.

It looks like June will not be testifying and, in fact, wants to come to California with him, and with the boys, when he is released. When he mentioned this on the telephone I said I thought it would be fine.

Enclosed is my letter to Judge Muszynski:

189

I am writing to you in regard to Jack Clouser, who will be a defendant in your court on December 2nd.

Jack is very frugal and budgets carefully. He found us a very nice three-room cottage in San Francisco for $70 a month, which is unheard of in this area. He likes to do the majority of the grocery shopping and keeps it simple and conservative. He has few clothes and doesn't buy any until the old ones are really worn out. In fact, other than sports clothes and work clothes, he owns one complete suit and that is the one I will be sending for him to wear in court. Because of this quality Jack has of being so frugal we have been able to build up a small savings and it is the first time in my life that I have had this feeling of security.

Jack is quite active socially and has many friends who respect him very much. There are at least 25 of his friends and acquaintances (besides his friends at the Eagle Club) who wanted to sign the security bond we anticipated would be forthcoming. . . .

Whatever circumstances he was in ten years ago must have been deplorable. Jack has never done anything that has not been honest all the years I have known him. He is a very good man who simply wants to earn a decent living and have a reasonably happy family life. . . . I pray that the court will not be deceived by these accusations and that his defense will succeed in freeing him so that he will be able to live the remaining years of his life in peace and love, which is all he truly desires.

Most sincerely,
Margaret Simons

December 6, 1974

DEAR DAVE,

Yesterday I pleaded guilty to a charge of conspiracy in the Cinema Theater robbery.

You can't believe how bad I wanted to go to trial, but not in Orange County. Not getting a change of venue beat me, plus being told *before* the trial what the sentence would be. The Judge said, "It will be thirty years if convicted, and once jury selection begins no lesser plea will be accepted. You have two minutes to decide." They also had Allie Brown there and he really believed it was my testimony that sent his brother to prison. So I accepted their offer and pled guilty to conspiracy. That carries a five-year sentence, but with time served

190

I'll be eligible for parole in six months. The most I can do is fourteen months.

Eagan said in the papers the next day, "It was brinksmanship. I feel we won holding a poker hand with a pair of deuces." They know they would have lost if they let me out of Orange County or even on bond where I could have talked to Brown and told him the truth. I couldn't risk thirty years away from the boys or Margy. I'm just as innocent now as I always was on the Cinema, I hope you can explain that.

As soon as I pled guilty June got drunk and called me and told me she had another boy friend and would file for divorce. Fine, I told her, you know what I really want, but I promised the boys otherwise. Now they are mad at her for not sticking by me, and I am relieved of my promise. They informed her, divorce or no divorce, they want to live with me!

Just imagine the hatred Brown has had for me for ten years, building year after year because of his belief that I was responsible for his brother being put away. I recently saw him on a TV show here in Orlando and he said, "It's not right for Jack to come back after all these years to fame and fortune," so maybe there's some jealousy involved too. In the end he wouldn't listen to Siff or Kirkland or June. He wanted to get even with me.

Six months! That's not all that bad. After what I've been through, I could do that in a closet. And then I'll be a totally free man. Think of that, a totally free man.

Your friend,
Jack